RISKING
AND RESISTING

Discovering the Untold Story of My Family's
Fight for Freedom in World War II

MARIE LE FEBVRE

www.riskingandresisting.com

www.marie-le-febvre.com

ISBN: 978-3-00-050749-6

Printed in the United States of America

First Printing 2015

Cover design by
JD&J Book Cover Design

Interior design by
Nand Kishore Pandey

RISKING AND RESISTING

"Never in my wildest dreams could I have imagined that a simple letter to the Le Febvre family would spark an emotional journey of discovery, joy, and surprise. I am delighted Marie was able to discover her family's courageous past, ordinary people taking extraordinary steps and the part they played in the struggle for freedom.

This is a touching, thoughtful and important book for our times. The history of the events that happened in France during World War II and the story of how members of our families met have been thoughtfully laid out for the reader."

—Amy Schmidt
Peachtree City, Georgia, U.S.

"As years pass by, we tend to forget that as sure as war means violence and chaos, risking and resisting surely takes courage and bravery, and leads to brotherhood and chance encounters. This book reminds us of what freedom is about and what it takes to keep it safe."

—Agathe de Saint Thomas
Paris, France

"This is an extraordinary story of heroism, courage, and friendship in occupied France during World War II. A remarkable tale based on a true story of American soldiers being rescued and hidden with great risk by French resistance fighters. A must read for anybody who is interested in history, daring bravery and lasting friendship. A truly amazing read!"

— Heinrich Senfft
Berlin, Germany

"A book about life in two different historical moments and places with one baseline: Fight for freedom. A tale about history and empathy, about family and love, about courage and fight.

It's worth reading it, not only for the understanding of the WWII but, above all, for the awareness that we are all connected."

—Ana Sanchez de Vivar
Berlin, Germany

This book taught me a lot about a side of the war that is unfortunately not very well known: how ordinary people became extraordinary citizens and played a tremendous part in the recovery of our freedom. Reading about their daily fight on the ground made me see WWII in a different light. A valuable read.

—Marie Capelle
Paris, France

Pour vous petits LE FEBVRE:
Teva, Lola, Atea,
Lucie, Manon,
and
CARL

RISKING AND RESISTING

CONTENTS

CHAPTER ONE

THE GROUND DISAPPEARS
Paris—April, 2013

I could feel the ground vanishing under my feet. And, with each ping in my inbox, another piece of earth fell away.

It was all too much to absorb: first one email, and then another, and another. During the next few hours, email after email continued to flood my inbox in random order, each with numerous attachments. All from a complete stranger who lived on the other side of the ocean. I began to read, but had to stop and catch my breath.

I slipped outside to the balcony of our Paris apartment and took in the quiet of the night. I craved fresh air, and needed to get lost in the infinite sky and hear the calming wind blow in the trees on the street below. Time seemed to float as I gazed at the stars from this magical place in the middle of the crowded city.

Eventually, my inbox drew me back inside. I stayed up all night poring over every word of more than fifty files. Seventy years of my family's history were unfolding with each document I read: dreams and disappointments, lives of hardship, and some happy moments.

At times, I felt as if I were invading the privacy of people I barely knew, but I couldn't pull myself away.

It had all started with a letter from this stranger …

CHAPTER TWO

THE LETTER
Paris—May 8, 2010

I wasn't thinking about war or acts of heroism as I navigated the road on that beautiful spring day in France, and I certainly never anticipated the intensely emotional journey that was to follow. May 8, 2010 was a national holiday, and I'd arranged to have a leisurely lunch with Maman at her home in Garches. As always, I looked forward to visiting my mother and enjoyed spending time in the house I grew up in. Situated between Paris and Versailles, Garches is only twelve kilometers from the capital, a short commute to the big city yet far enough away to retain a unique rural flavor—the best of both worlds.

Maman and I sat down to lunch as we'd done many times before and enjoyed the simple salad and cheese plate she'd prepared. We French have a reputation for being excellent cooks, but somehow Maman had never mastered a high degree of culinary skill. This was a source of great amusement among my siblings and me, and we delighted in joking about her latest concoctions, like her indisputably famous cucumber ice cream. I was a bit disappointed that my sister, Maud, was unable to join us. She and her husband, Lionel, live in Garches with their two daughters, Lucie and Manon, and they were on a family holiday. We would have had some fun teasing Maman about the many strange dishes we'd consumed at her table over the years.

Maman and I engaged in our usual discussion about family, the weather, and other items of interest. She clearly had something else on her mind that she wished to discuss with me, and she brought it up in her own good time. She'd recently received a letter addressed to her and my papa, who'd passed away fourteen years earlier in 1996.

"Since your English is better than anyone else's in the family, it would be best if you take care of this," said Maman, handing me an envelope.

I pulled out a folded sheet of paper and began to read.

Dear Mr. and Mrs. Le Febvre,

I wanted to inform you of our loss. My dad, Russell Cotts, has passed away. He died in December of last year.

I have been looking through my dad's war history, memorabilia and letters when I came upon letters from you. I realized you were the son of Claude Le Febvre and grandson of his mother Christiane Le Febvre.

I want you to know my dad always remembered and was extremely grateful to your grandparents and your father, Claude, for the sacrifices and danger they put themselves in on his behalf. He never forgot. And he always spoke highly of your family and those of the French Resistance.

He referred to your family as "the most courageous people in the world."

I will always remember as a child how happy and excited he was when he received a letter from your grandmother or Claude.

I want you to know he loved them very, very much.

Sincerely,

Amy Cotts Schmidt

I examined the envelope and its contents once again and discovered that Amy Schmidt had written the letter a month earlier, and the return address indicated she lived in Peachtree City, Georgia. A second piece of paper was included in the envelope: Russell Cotts' obituary. He'd served in World War II (WWII) as an aircraft commander and pilot in the 385th Bomb Group with the U.S. Army Air Forces in Europe. Mr. Cotts' plane was shot down during a mission, but he evaded capture by the German Army with the help of members of the French Resistance.

My head was spinning, and I felt a strange twinge in the pit of my stomach as I tried to make sense of all of this. *French Resistance? The most courageous people in the world? Were this American woman and the accompanying obituary referring to members of my family?* I looked at Maman.

"Do you know what this is about?" I asked.

Maman merely shook her head. I suppose that's no surprise. In general, we French are private people. We don't ask a lot of questions of one another, nor do we volunteer much information. My mother is especially private and has a saying, "Chacun son jardin secret." Literally translated, it means "Each of us has our secret garden."

I sat for a moment, the letter in my hand, as a distant memory stirred in my thoughts. When I was a child growing up in Garches, my paternal and maternal grandparents lived next door to one another, just across the street from my parents' house. (It was an ideal situation for me, and in my imagination, I pictured my parents as teenagers, carrying on flirtatious conversations as they leaned out the windows of their respective homes.) Great-grandmother Christiane and her husband, Great-grandfather Georges, whom we called "Grand-père à Chapeau" (Grandfather with a hat), also lived across the street. I have vague memories of Grand-père à Chapeau: He was an elegant gentleman from the old French aristocracy. But, for whatever reason, I have no recollection at all of Great-grandmother Christiane.

Papa's parents also had a home in Normandy, but when they were in Garches, they often popped in to chat before dinner. During one of those visits, Grand-père Claude mentioned that one of his American friends from the war had been searching for him. When the American couldn't locate my grandfather, he contacted the weekly newspaper in Rambouillet, the town where Grand-père lived during the war, to ask for their help.

I was only nine years old at the time, but I recall how touched my grandfather was that the American pilot had gone to such lengths to find him. As a child, I really knew nothing of World War II, but the unique friendship Grand-père had formed with someone from the other side of the Atlantic fascinated me. Unfortunately, my grandfather didn't offer further details, and no one asked. Unlike my grandmother, who was a chatterbox, my grandfather was more a listener than a talker.

Now, after reading Amy Schmidt's letter these many years later, I put two and two together and assumed the pilot who'd been searching for Grand-père Claude was Russell Cotts. I asked Maman what else she knew of Grandfather's story, but she knew no more than I did. We couldn't ask my grandfather because, sadly, he and my father had passed away within six months of each other. I suggested to Maman that Uncle Patrice, my father's brother, would be the best person to respond to the letter. She agreed, as Uncle Patrice was the only member of Papa's family who was still alive. She also promised to go through the box of my papa's papers—a box that had remained unopened for fifteen years—to see what she could find.

The journey back to Paris that afternoon was very different than the one to my mother's house earlier in the day. Traffic was horrendous, and the drive took twice as long as it normally did. Oddly, though, I was grateful for the extra time behind the wheel because I needed to sort through my feelings. My comfortable, familiar world had shifted on its axis with a few strokes of a pen. *How bizarre life can be*, I thought. *A woman on the other side of the ocean has written to my mother and my dead father regarding something my family knows nothing about—not Maman, my siblings, or me. Why? Why don't we know anything?*

I was puzzled because I had been very close to Grand-père. When I was growing up, French schools dismissed early every Wednesday, and I established a particular routine with both sets of grandparents. I took the train to school, and my grandparents' homes were conveniently located about halfway between the train station and my parents' home; so, I often visited them. First, I stopped to eat lunch with my mother's parents. Unlike Maman, my grandmother was an excellent cook, and I enjoyed her special dishes that simmered for hours over a low flame. My grandfather firmly believed that "an apple a day keeps the doctor away," but his apple was in the form of a delectable, warm apple tart. My mouth watered in anticipation each time I walked from the train station to their home because I knew I was in for a tasty treat.

After lunch, I walked next door to visit Grand-père Claude and my grandmother Jeannine, whose nickname was "Manine." Grand-père always used to say, "Venir prendre le café après ton déjeuner." ("Come have coffee after lunch.") It's a common saying in France, similar to "Come and have a drink." I'd usually find Grand-père sitting and reading or working on his *mots-croisés* (crossword puzzles), a cup of coffee and a smoldering cigarette on the table beside him. I have extraordinary memories of those afternoons: We drank the most delicious mint tea made with fresh spearmint from the garden. (Manine was fortunate to have travelled the world, and learned the tradition of mint tea in North Africa.) I loved watching Grand-père or Manine preparing the tea. A huge bunch of fresh mint, black tea, and loads of sugar were carefully placed in a beautiful teapot that resembled Aladdin's lamp. When the tea was sufficiently steeped, Grand-père ceremoniously raised the teapot as high as he possibly could, and poured equal amounts of tea into three brightly-colored glasses, never spilling so much as a drop.

"Why do you lift the teapot so high?" I used to ask.

"To bring air into the mixture," Grand-père replied.

I've tried over and over again to make this same tea, but I'm never successful at pouring it from such a height without spilling it. The last step in crafting this exquisite drink was to add a sprinkling of pine nuts, which floated on top. The tea was so hot, we often had to wait fifteen minutes before we could drink it. And then, we'd while away the time discussing anything and everything from books to philosophy to travel. But Grand-père never mentioned the war.

An enormous sense of loss and sadness washed over me as I thought about this amazing man with whom I shared so much. He even took time to teach me how to drive and to change a tire. I must admit, I wasn't the easiest of students to teach, but he was exceedingly patient and brave! Wouldn't he be proud to see me driving like a pro—in horrendous traffic, no less—as I made my way back to Paris? A single tear escaped down my cheek as I also thought about my dear Papa, who passed away only a few days before my twentieth birthday. I wasn't yet an adult, and I would have loved so much to have shared all my thoughts and dreams with him. As each tear blended into the next, I allowed myself to grieve. *How sad that Grand-père never talked about his experience in the war. How sad it is that Papa is not here anymore. I miss them both so much.*

I arrived in Paris, late for dinner at my partner Sascha's apartment. Of course, being late is the norm for Parisians, but Sascha is Austrian and always punctual. When I arrived, he teased me because I was late yet again. He asked about my journey to the countryside and I used one of his favorite English expressions to respond. "Very interesting," I said, and handed him the letter.

"Well, I guess there really were members of the French Resistance during the war," he said, somewhat jokingly. "I'm surprised you haven't talked about this before."

"I never mentioned it because I had no idea myself. And now there are so many unanswered questions."

We toasted with glasses of Prosecco, a delicious Italian sparkling white wine. (As a French woman, I'm supposed to prefer Champagne, but truth be told, I love Prosecco.) We clinked glasses and Sascha said, "To the real patriots. Those from today and those we know nothing about."

I contacted Uncle Patrice a couple of days later. My family had had little contact with him over the years because Patrice lived on the seashore in Normandy and was somewhat of a recluse; however, since he was the only family member left who could possibly know anything about Russell Cotts, I telephoned him. I was thrilled when Uncle Patrice told me he remembered Cotts was an American pilot hidden by my great-grandmother at my great-grandparents' home in Rambouillet during the war. I had naturally assumed Cotts was the pilot Grand-père had talked about that afternoon at our home when I was nine years old, but to my surprise, Uncle Patrice said he was not. *Claude Le Febvre, my beloved grandfather, had more than one American pilot friend? And his mother—my Great-grandmother Christiane—hid these American pilots?*

Uncle Patrice agreed to answer Amy Schmidt's letter after I assured him I'd immediately send him a copy and would give him the original the next time I visited Normandy. At that time, I often made the trip to Trouville-sur-Mer, a small village along the coast of Normandy, because my father's ashes had been scattered there and breathing in the salty sea air gave me a sense of comfort and peace. It was only two hours from Paris, so I went whenever I could, every two months or so. In fact, my family established a ritual to honor my father each year on the anniversary of his death: Every November 4, Maman, my brother, my sister, and I, along with our families, went there to have lunch beside the sea. My brother, Yann, is three years older than I and lives on Reunion Island in the Indian Ocean with his wife, Alexandra, and their three children, Teva, Lola, and Atea. Although traveling to Trouville-sur-Mer requires a lengthy flight, Yann and his family come whenever they can.

I naturally assumed I'd see Patrice during one of my frequent visits and would have the opportunity to learn more of the story. Unfortunately, my uncle became even more reclusive, and I never saw him again.

True to my word, I sent a copy of the letter to Uncle Patrice, and then for the time being, I forgot all about it.

CHAPTER THREE

TOUTES LES NOUVELLES
Garches—2010, a few months later

Although I'd allowed thoughts of my family's past to slip out of my mind, my curiosity returned when, a couple of months later, Maman gave me a file she'd found among some papers in the cellar. She opened boxes that had remained untouched for years, and pulled out whatever documents she could find that related to Grand-père. We're not the most organized family, and I suspect Maman had to wade through all kinds of papers and photos that had been indiscriminately tossed into boxes. I'm certain it wasn't easy for her to revisit the past; it's not easy for any of us to be reminded of happier times when Papa was alive and then of the terrible moment when he died suddenly.

The file Maman gave me contained an old newspaper article, a few pictures, and a crumpled typewritten note. The article was a follow-up to an item that had appeared in the March 30, 1988 edition of the city of Rambouillet's weekly newspaper, *Toutes Les Nouvelles* (*All the News*). I finally had something concrete that connected my family to a mysterious past!

It wasn't surprising that I found the first link to this unknown chapter of my family's past in Rambouillet: The city is rich with history, and Christiane and her husband, Georges, lived in Rambouillet with their two sons. Both Grand-père Claude and Manine grew up in Rambouillet and lived there as young adults. This small city is located approximately twenty-five miles southwest of Paris (just a thirty-five minute train ride from our capital), and is probably known most for its historic castle, the Château de Rambouillet, constructed in the fourteenth century. Until 2009, it was the official summer residence of the president of the French Republic. Numerous international conferences have been held there, and foreign statesmen are often hosted at this castle. Before the revolution of 1789, it was owned by King Louis XVI, who commissioned the building of a *laterie* (dairy), to appease his wife, Marie Antoinette, who found the château to be boring. Rambouillet became part of the German occupied zone during WWII, and the Germans requisitioned the castle as a residence for high-ranking officers. General Charles de Gaulle of France used the château as his headquarters just before the liberation of Paris. Today, visitors from around the world—and indeed the French themselves—go to Rambouillet to visit the château, its surrounding gardens and park.

The story in the Rambouillet newspaper described a former American airman's efforts to find the family that had hidden him after he'd been shot down by the Germans during WWII. They had lived in Rambouillet, and saved his life by sheltering him until the Liberation. Forty-four years had passed, and retired Air Force Colonel Jack Davis hoped to see his rescuers once again.

The family Davis sought was *my family!* My great-grandmother, Christiane Le Febvre, and her son Claude, my grandfather.

Within hours of publication, a journalist was speaking to my grandfather by telephone. Grand-père no longer lived in Rambouillet, but his brother-in-law read the article and immediately got in touch with the newspaper. The follow-up piece appeared in the next edition of *Toutes Les Nouvelles.*

April 6, 1988

Forty-Four Years Later, Fate Brings Them Together

By S. Désenclos

*It's a beautiful story. There are days when it is very reward-
ing to work as a journalist. Thanks to you, the readers of our
newspaper, two men whom fate had brought together back in
1944—and were separated at the moment of the liberation of
France—will meet again after forty-four years.*

*Last Wednesday, we told the moving story of a young American
soldier whose plane was shot down by the Germans on August
2, 1944—and who had been hidden by some residents of Rambouillet until Liberation. Forty-four years later, that soldier, retired U.S. Air Force Colonel Jack Davis, was desperately looking
for the family that had hidden him for seventeen days.*

*Thanks to the many responses following last week's article,
Claude Le Febvre, who during the war lived at 44, rue du Petit-
Parc in Rambouillet, was found in less than twenty-four hours.
We first spoke with Le Febvre by telephone. At the mention of
the name Davis, Claude Le Febvre's voice changed. "Jack? Jack
Davis?" That same evening, our reporter met with Le Febvre at
his home in Garches, where he modestly shared the story of his
activity with the Comet Line[1], and summer evenings when he
played cards with Americans while listening to the BBC.*

The Comet Line

*"From the day of the landing, my mother and I enlisted in the
Comet Line," said Le Febvre, arranging his photo albums while
deep-rooted memories from more than forty years before be-*

---

1 The Comet Line ("Le Réseau Comète), was a Resistance group started in Belgium. Its purpose was to help fallen airmen return to Allied control.

gan to surface. "We lived on rue du Petit Parc in Rambouillet. The Comet line brought us Allied troop officers who needed to hide." Initially, there were some English and then a New Zealander who found refuge with Le Febvre. Some stayed for a long time; others were quickly evacuated to the Chevreuse Valley, dressed as firemen. In early August, four Americans arrived at Le Febvre's home: They had all been aboard a B-17 Flying Fortress that was shot down—presumably above Trappes—where the Germans had installed powerful anti-aircraft guns. Recovered by Eugène Falenpein, they found themselves at the home of Christiane Le Febvre, who lived in a five-bedroom home in Rambouillet with her youngest son, Claude. Jack Davis and Jans Lindquist would remain at the Le Febvre home until the liberation of Rambouillet.

Exhilarating Times—The Days Passed Quickly

"Life at that time was exhilarating and the days passed quickly," said Claude Le Febvre. "The Americans spent their time listening to the BBC and playing cards. Occasionally, we walked in the gardens which were sheltered by the high shrubs surrounding the house." Sometimes, the Germans searched for the Americans. (When they shot down a [Boeing B-17] Flying Fortress, the Germans counted the corpses and thus knew the exact number of fugitive soldiers.) At no time were the soliders left alone. It was too dangerous in case of a routine check," said Jeannine Le Febvre, Claude's fiancée, who kept the Americans company when Christiane and Claude Le Febvre were absent.

Before the War, Jack Davis Was a Professional Jazz Drummer

Claude and Jeannine Le Febvre have fond memories of the period that followed the Allied landing on the beaches of Normandy. "Before the war, Jack Davis was a professional jazz drummer," said Claude. "When he began to play drums with his fingers it was unbelievable!" Jeannine and Claude Le Febvre also remember the day when they went out to dinner and sat with other

French who were "anti-Nazi" and eager to have the Americans at their table. "Coming back just before the curfew, we passed in front of the German Kommandant's Headquarters. The Americans laughed at the idea of passing in front of the guards without the Germans having any idea about their real identities."

It was very emotional for both the Americans and the Le Febvres when it came time for the Americans to depart after the liberation of Rambouillet. "They insisted on buying French perfume to bring home to the other side of the Atlantic. I tried to tell them the perfume made during the war wasn't any good, but they didn't want to listen!"

As he was leaving with his comrades for Paris, Jack Davis gave his watch to Christiane Le Febvre as a souvenir of their time together. When his mother passed away, Claude Le Febvre found the sergeant's gift; he kept it carefully tucked away, unaware that one day he would have the opportunity to bring it out for such an occasion.

Nobody really knows why on the other side of the Atlantic, forty-four years later, the U.S. Air Force officer set his mind to finding those who saved him from falling into the hands of the Germans. Like many other retired American officers, Jack Davis began to search for his past. Here in France, nobody blames all the soldiers of the Allied forces for their more than forty years of silence. On learning that Jack Davis was trying to find him to invite him to the United States, Claude Le Febvre was moved and touched. He talked about his memories of this time with great humility. Even when discussing how he risked being shot, he remained modest.[2]

I was delighted to finally discover the identity of the airman who'd searched for my grandfather, and amazed that Jack Davis had sought out Grand-père after so many years. As I carefully put the newspaper

2 Article translated and included with permission of *Les Nouvelles de Versailles*.

article on the table beside me, my mind became a tangle of rushing thoughts. *I thought I knew Grand-père so well … but I had no idea about any of this. He was incredibly brave. I never even knew my great-grandmother's first name. Christiane must have been an extremely courageous woman to hide those pilots in her home. Both Grand-père and Christiane put their lives in danger—all in the name of freedom.*

With the significance of the Rambouillet newspaper article still sinking in, I turned my attention to the partial note Maman had also found. The paper was extremely thin, almost transparent, and reminiscent of the paper used years ago for airmail letters. It was so fragile that it had been mostly destroyed. "Note Concerning Madame Christiane Le Febvre" was typed across the top in capital letters. However, the letter-size piece of paper had been carefully torn right across the middle of the page, leaving me with just the top half of one page of this "note," which seemed to be an official letter from the Resistance. At the top of the letter was a brief handwritten notation, "Here, my dear friend, is the copy of the note about you, sent by your friend L. Constantin." It was signed "Respectfully," but the signature was not legible. This half-note was confusing to me, and I wondered about the great-grandmother I never knew.

NOTE CONCERNING Madame Christiane LE FEBVRE

Everyone who knew the dangers that Madame Christiane Le Febvre gallantly and calmly faced during the Occupation was surprised and displeased to learn that the commission of Attribution for the Medal of the Resistance did not feel Madame Le Febvre was deserving of a medal.

Given her actions, it is painful to see a French woman, honored by the Allied nations England and the United States, but not her own country. It is true that it is not the Medal of the Resistance that she should receive, but the Cross of the Legion of Honor.

As proof, we offer the following evidence:

1.) *The records of Claude Le Febvre, son of Madame Le Febvre, state: "A young and ardent patriot, who actively assisted his mother in the hosting and repatriation of Allied airmen."*

2.) *A September 15, 1944 document from the Comet Line indicates that Madame Christiane Le Febvre "was of great value in housing downed Allied airmen, and carried out her mission with the utmost courage until the Liberation."*

The note filled me with pride—yet also puzzled me. *If the Allies acknowledged Christiane's heroism, why didn't she receive the same recognition from France? She was incredibly brave. She took care of all those Americans at her home. Could my great-grandmother possibly have done something wrong?*

Growing up in the 1980s, I was taught that General de Gaulle was a WWII hero, and either you were a "good French person," loyal to de Gaulle and his fight for the liberation of France, or you were part of the *Collabos,* the term used for those French who collaborated with the Germans. *Could Great-grandmother Christiane have been a Collabo? Is that why she didn't receive a medal from France?*

Although I was curious about the reasons Great-grandmother Christiane's own country would neglect to acknowledge her valor, at the time I received the file from my mother, my own life was in transition—and I wasn't ready to face the past, especially if it meant I had a "Collabo Great-grandmother." So once again I pushed my newfound knowledge into the background. I needed to focus on my future.

My life really was a bit of a mess back then. I was thirty-three, had a new man in my life following the end of my ten-year marriage the year before, and had no real place of my own to call home. Sascha worked a job that required equal amounts of time living in New York and Paris. When he was in Paris, I stayed at his apartment as often as possible. I spent the remainder of my time living in my brother's empty home in Ville d'Avray, near Garches. I maintained a nomadic lifestyle, and carried my clothes and my most treasured possessions in a small suitcase in the trunk of my car. And, I had a highly stressful job working for a large international company: I am a creative perfumer, or a "nose" as we are called in France. In fact, when I was thirty years old, I got my pilot's license so I could more easily travel to obscure locations to seek out unique raw materials for creating perfumes.

Flying has also helped me find myself, but I didn't realize my ability to fly a plane would also give me insight into the past that I, for the time being, had laid aside.

CHAPTER FOUR

WORLD WAR II: THE BACKDROP BEHIND THE STORY

Discovering a personal connection to events that happened so many years ago—and my relationship with Sascha—provided me with the incentive to conduct my own research into WWII. Sascha's interest in the war is deeply personal: His father, an Austrian, was incarcerated in the U.S. as a prisoner of war. As our relationship grew, Sascha and I spent hours together watching movies and documentaries about the war and sharing our individual perspectives with each other and our diverse circle of friends. Looking back, I now realize I knew very little then. I'd been an above-average student, but what I'd learned about WWII in school barely scratched the surface. The fact that the war was a "touchy" subject in my country never even entered my mind! Researching on the Internet, reading books, and engaging in a free exchange with my Austrian, German, English, and American acquaintances really helped me understand the whole picture.

For many of my countrymen, talking about the war was taboo, so I only learned the basic facts that were taught in school. But I knew numerous people were still bitter decades after the war had ended. My childhood best friend, Annabelle, was half-German and half-French, and I vividly recall how much she suffered because of her German heritage. In the eighties the Germans were still not very welcome in France, not even a little girl. Children were very rude to Annabelle and often repeated to her the words their parents and grandparents had said at home. I know she was extremely hurt, and am sure her parents moved her to the German school for this reason, among others. However, despite witnessing these instances of unkind behavior, I was still very naïve about the war and lacked any knowledge about its global scope.

Unfortunately, I believe many individuals of my generation and those younger share my lack of information and understanding. The passage of time often results in diminishing interest in historical and social events and blurs our perception of their relevance. Because of this, I suspect one day the general populace will know as little about WWII as most of my contemporaries do about the Roman Empire. We may have gotten away with knowing little about wars that occurred early in our history, but today it's crucial that everyone on the face of the planet understand the causes and consequences of this global war in order to prevent it from happening again. Modern society is much more complicated and fragile, and events that occur in one part of the globe—conflict in the Middle East, for example, or the creation of Israel as an independent state—can influence the course of history. So it's important to study our recent past, to really learn from our ancestors' mistakes and successes.

My opinion is based, in part, on discussions I've had with others while writing this book. I remember mentioning my project to my nieces and nephews and was quite taken aback when one said, "Oh yes, Hitler was the bad guy who killed Jews and blonds." Of course, they're children—the eldest was no more than thirteen at the time—but their responses made me clearly realize that, if I didn't do something to help others learn more about the war, my nieces and nephews might grow up with the same lack of understanding and misconceptions as I. Most schools equip students only with basic knowledge. At that moment, I decided a timeline and a brief history of the war might help readers put the events I've written about into context.

In the United States, Great Britain, Western Europe, and many nations throughout the world, we are *free*: We enjoy the freedom to live as we wish as long as we abide by certain rules of behavior, and most of us can't imagine living any other way. But war, especially when it's staged on your own soil, changes everything. It creates nightmarish conditions, which alter every aspect of a person's existence. Just ask the French.

The Great War, as WWI is called, lasted for four years, and much of the war on the Western front was fought on French soil, where the Germans appeared to have the upper hand. Northern French residents who lived under German control along the Belgian border during WWI had their food, supplies, and possessions requisitioned, their travel restricted, and their information censored. Every liberty they'd once enjoyed was seized and these peaceful people were forced to endure the harshest conditions imaginable. Malnutrition, sickness, and disease were rampant, and Germans ordered the deportation and evacuation of many civilians from the homes they'd lived in their entire lives.

In July 1918, however, the Allies forced German troops to retreat, and then launched a powerful counteroffensive that struck a deadly blow to the enemy. The French commander-in-chief, Marshal Philippe Pétain, led the Allies' advance and was instrumental in achieving an absolute victory. On November 11, 1918, Germany formally surrendered and, two months later, representatives from approximately thirty nations traveled to Versailles to attend the Paris Peace Conference. Their sole purpose was to determine terms of peace for Europe following the war. The Treaty of Versailles, signed in June 1919, imposed strict sanctions on Germany, which included disarmament and territorial clauses. German representatives also were required to sign a "War Guilt Clause," indicating Germany was responsible for starting WWI and, as such, was liable for all material damages.

German citizens resented the harsh terms of the treaty, which turned their lives into a daily struggle for survival. During the months following the Armistice, Germans were forced to live under a blockade, and more than a quarter million citizens perished from starvation and disease. These wretched conditions added fuel to the fire: Many felt alienated from the political leaders who governed them, and a large segment of the population became further disenfranchised during the late 1920s and early 1930s when economic depression dominated their lives, paving the way for charismatic Adolf Hitler and his Nazi Party. Hitler was elected Chancellor of Germany in 1933.

November 11, 1918	End of World War I – Germany surrenders. France, with 39.6 million citizens, lost 1.4 million soldiers and 300,000 civilians, and 4,266,000 military members were wounded.[3] November 11 is now celebrated as a national holiday in France.
June 28, 1919	WWI officially ends with the signing of the Treaty of Versailles by the Allied Nations and Germany.
July 21, 1921	Hitler becomes leader of the National Socialist (Nazi) Party.
January 30, 1933	Hitler becomes Chancellor of Germany.
March/June 1933	The first two concentration camps are opened.[4]
July 1933	The Nazi Party is declared the only legal political party in Germany. (The Nazi state is also referred to as the Third Reich.)
August 19, 1934	Hitler becomes Führer[5] of Germany.
August 1939	Germany (under Nazi dictator Adolf Hitler) and the Soviet Union (under Communist dictator Joseph Stalin) sign the Nonaggression Pact, which secretly accepts Germany's plan to invade Poland.[6]
September 1939	Nazis invades Poland; Britain and France declare war on Germany, and WWII begins.

---

3 (2015). Armistice of 11 November 1918. Retrieved from http://www.france.fr/en/institutions-and-values/armistice-11-november-1918.html

4 The first prisoners were political opponents; Communists, Jews, homosexuals, intellectuals, and other "threats" to Hitler's ideology were also imprisoned.

5 The literal translation of "führer" is "leader" or "guide." In the case of Hitler, he became both chancellor and president combined.

6 National Geographic Society. (2015). Pearl Harbor World War II Timeline. Retrieved from http://www.nationalgeographic.com/pearlharbor/history/wwii_timeline.htmlp

The precise causes of the war are extremely complex, but instabilities in Europe and elsewhere after WWI contributed to increasingly explosive political tension in and among nations. Western European nations were increasingly concerned about the threat of Communism, and they viewed Germany as the last barrier between them and Soviet expansion. (After WWII, tensions between Western and Soviet ideology would result in the Cold War.) In 1939, German troops invaded Poland under Hitler's orders. Great Britain and France quickly responded by declaring war on Germany. And once again, countries around the globe became polarized, as two opposing alliances—the Allies and the Axis Powers—fought. Great Britain, the United States, China, and the Soviet Union were foremost among the Allies; the principal Axis nations included Germany, Japan, and Italy.

Although the United States was initially reluctant to join the fighting, the Japanese bombing of Pearl Harbor in December 1941 led to a change of heart; and ultimately, America's entry changed the war's course in both the Pacific and Atlantic arenas. By 1943, British and American forces defeated the Italians and Germans in North Africa. An Allied invasion of Sicily and Italy followed—though Allied fighting against the Germans in Italy would continue until 1945.

World War II (1939-1945) covered six continents and resulted in an estimated 45-60 million deaths (military and civilian), including over six million Jews.

France During WWII

France was no stranger to war. Its armed forces and staunch citizens had held out against the Germans for four long years during WWI, and no other country's losses equaled the number of French deaths: 1.3 million of its people perished. But France was a different nation when Germany invaded in 1940. Paul Reynaud headed the government, and though he held out hope that France could emerge victorious, he soon resigned under pressure by defeatists in his cabinet. Reynaud's vice-premier was none other than WWI hero Marshal Philippe Pétain, who took over as premier when Reynaud resigned.

The beloved eighty-four-year-old immediately asked Germany to provide terms for France's surrender. An armistice was signed on June 22, which divided France into two regions: the German occupied zone (the north of France as well as the western coast), and the non-occupied south of France, which remained under French control with a new government that was set up by Pétain in the spa town of Vichy. France, a great military power two decades earlier, had surrendered to the Germans in six short weeks.

France after the Armistice June 22, 1940

Four months later, Pétain announced he was entering into collaboration with Hitler. French citizens were divided about this new turn of events: Many were loyal to Pétain and supported his action. He was, they reasoned, a respected elder statesman who championed the correct strategy. Others, however, were horrified that an armistice with the Nazis had been achieved. They were convinced the country could have fought longer and harder. These individuals were determined to do just that—to continue the fight, to *resist* the Germans, to become *résistants*. With great resolve and courage the French Resistance was born.

In November 1942, Germany invaded the unoccupied zone of France in response to Allied landings in North Africa, and Pétain became nothing more than a figurehead. Travel was restricted, curfews imposed, newspapers censored, and ID cards issued. Life was even more difficult in heavily-populated French cities and along the coast, where larger populations of Germans dwelled. Citizens waited in endless lines to buy food, which was rationed, and many basic necessities were unavailable. Confronted with a bleak future, individuals faced three choices: resist, collaborate, or do nothing.

I believe it's important for me to take a moment to explain how uncomfortable most French are with the topic of WWII. Even though the war is long over, it's not something we like to discuss. Of course, French history classes address the war, but until I started conducting my own research, what I'd learned in school had always served as truth: namely, that Pétain and his Vichy government, and *no one else,* were responsible for handing over France to the Germans. I blindly believed this to be correct because it's what I was taught. Sascha helped me see otherwise, rather than believing a hundred percent of what I read, and encouraged me to search for all the answers.

Once I started investigating, I learned that collaboration against the Jews in WWII by anyone other than Vichy wasn't publicly discussed for five decades, but it certainly occurred. In 1995, shortly after taking office, President Jacques Chirac openly acknowledged France's responsibility for deporting thousands of Jews to Nazi death camps during the German occupation in WWII. He gave this speech on the fifty-third anniversary of the *Vel' d'Hiv Roundup* in Paris, which occurred on July 12, 1942, during which French police helped round up more than 13,000 Jews. They were then crammed into a cycling stadium before being deported to death camps.

While WWII is a dark period in the history of my country, and remains a taboo subject for some, I am so proud to have discovered the roles played by my ancestors. They *resisted*. My great-grandmother and Grand-père were résistants. Like their fellow résistants, they believed, not in a German-occupied France, but in a free country. And they were willing to fight for that freedom no matter the cost.

D-Day, the Allied Invasion of Normandy

I remember reading about World War II in grade school and learning that D-Day—June 6, 1944—was one of the most important dates in the battle against Germany. On that particular day, more than 160,000 Allied troops stormed the northern coast of France to fight the Germans on the beaches of Normandy. The invasion of this area of France continued for more than two months, into August 1944.

From the moment the United States entered the war, the Allies focused on defeating Germany: Their strategy was a massive invasion of northwest Europe. Formal planning for this attack began in 1943, and a target date was set for the spring of 1944. American General Dwight D. Eisenhower was appointed Supreme Commander of the Allied Expeditionary Forces, and he and six other Allied commanders planned the details of what would become the largest air, land, and sea operation undertaken before, or since, June 6, 1944. The top-secret mission, code-named Operation Overlord, involved landing nine divisions of sea and airborne troops—over 5,000 ships, 11,000 airplanes, and 160,000 men—along a sixty-mile stretch of the French coast in the span of just twenty-four hours. Forces were to land on five beaches, secure their positions, and progress inland.

The operation was launched as planned, and by nightfall on June 6, Allied forces had established a large-scale lodgment in Normandy. There is no official number of casualties for D-Day, but it is estimated that approximately 10,400 Allied troops were wounded, and more than 4,000 died. During the days and weeks that followed, Allied troops continued to press inland, liberating French towns—including Rambouillet—as they went. The war finally ended with Germany's surrender on May 7, 1945.

May 10, 1940	The Nazi army, the army of the Third Reich, invades France.
June 14, 1940	Nazis enter Paris.
June 16, 1940	Pétain becomes President of the Council of Ministers.
June 22, 1940	France signs armistice with Germany.
November 11, 1942	Germans invade unoccupied France.
June 6, 1944	D-Day, the start of the campaign to defeat the Germans and liberate Europe.
August 16-19, 1944	Rambouillet is liberated.
August 25, 1944	Paris is liberated; Allied troops continue eastward.
May 1945	End of WWII in Europe.
	May 7: Nazi Germany signs unconditional surrender (at Allied headquarters in Reims, France) to take effect the following day. The British Commonwealth celebrates VE (Victory in Europe) Day.
	May 8: The United States and many European countries celebrate VE Day.
	May 9: Victory Day in former Soviet Union.

CHAPTER FIVE

AN AIRMAN'S TALE

I suppose it's a bit ironic that a year after meeting Sascha, I found out a little about my own family's involvement in the war through Amy's letter and Maman's discovery of the Rambouillet newspaper article about Jack Davis' search for Grand-père. I marveled at this American's determination to find Grand-père after more than four decades. When I had the opportunity to read Jack Davis' personal account of being shot down while his B-17 bomber was on a mission over France, I began to truly understand the personal sacrifices made by those who fought for freedom.

The crew of a B-17 bomber typically included ten men: four officers (the pilot, co-pilot, bombardier, and navigator) and six enlisted men (those ranked below officer in the chain of command). They were the flight engineer/top turret gunner, radio operator/flexible gunner, two waist gunners (right and left), tail gunner, and ball turret gunner. While flying any combat mission was perilous for all crew members, ball turret gunner Jack Davis served in one of the most dangerous capacities on the B-17 bomber. He manned two machine guns located in a small compartment—which could be accessed solely with help from the other crewmen—beneath the belly of the plane. There was just one way in and one way out of the ball turret: through a narrow hatch that could be opened only when the guns faced straight downward. Because the compartment and its entry were so tiny, ball turret gunners, also known as belly gunners, had to fight without their parachutes. Ball turret gunners were usually the shortest members of their crew—Jack Davis was five feet four inches tall. They were more vulnerable to enemy gunfire than other crew members, and it wasn't unusual for these men to suffer severe injuries or die—particularly when the plane's landing gear was damaged and the pilot had to make a belly landing.[7]

At the beginning of the war, B-17 crews were required to complete twenty-five combat missions before reassignment to the States, but right before Davis and five of his fellow crewmen reached that goal, the guidelines were changed. To compensate for a shortage of combat-ready bomber crews, General Jimmy Doolittle, commander of the powerful Eighth Air Force with its 42,000 combat aircraft, increased the mandated number of combat missions. Doolittle offered two choices to crews that had completed twenty-five combat missions: They could opt to go home for thirty days' leave, head back to combat for another twenty-five missions, and then return stateside permanently. Or, they could choose to fly ten more missions without taking leave. Once finished, they'd return home for good. Davis and his crew elected to fulfill the extra ten missions without a break so they could get back to the U.S. that much sooner.

Davis and his enlisted crew had completed twenty-five combat missions together—all with the same pilot. But, when crews were completing their additional ten missions, they weren't assigned to any particular pilot. The airmen had to seek out bomber planes in need of an enlisted crew in order to meet their quota. Davis' crew members were taking a well-deserved rest break when they were called as a fill-in crew.[8]

---

7 Explanation courtesy of Jimmy C. Davis, son of Jack Davis, who believes the ball turret gunner to have been the scariest position on a B-17 bomber.
8 Explanation courtesy of Jimmy C. Davis, son of Jack Davis.

Of the dozens of missions Sergeant Davis flew during the war, this mission—his thirty-second—was the most memorable. Forty years later, he wrote this account for his children and grandchildren.

August 2, 1944

Mission n° 32

385th Bomb Group – 551st Bomb Squadron

By Jack Davis

It was one-thirty in the morning of August 2nd, 1944, when a Sergeant entered the barracks and flipped on the lights. "Panasuk, Church, Waterfield, Abbott, Davis," he bellowed out. "Up and at 'em. You go today."

This would be my thirty-second mission. I'd heard this rude awakening thirty-one times before, not counting the missions that were called off because of weather. We looked forward to the red flare which cancelled flights. I suppose that on every mission—except the first one, when you don't know what to expect—you can't help but wonder if this is to be your last.

I reread some of Jerry's letters, and smiled as I thought of her safe at home with our little daughter. These were cherished moments before each mission. I noticed other airmen, not just our crew, looking at pictures and reading letters. I was not alone.

Those of us who were to fly out ate some meat, given its lack of tendency to cause gas. (Your stomach blows up like a balloon as you reach high altitude.) Then, at 3:00 a.m., we reported to the briefing room to receive our target for the day: an airfield just northeast of Paris. This particular airfield was being used by the German Luftwaffe [Air Force] to undermine our forces in Normandy. It seemed to be an easy mission, given the relatively short distance from our base to the target.

Little did I know then that my thirty-second mission would be my last.

We were a crew of five. I can't remember why our sixth crew member wasn't flying that day. We reported to the armorer to pick up our .50 caliber machine guns, and immediately moved on to the parachute hut to claim our chutes. Hoisting our weapons, we reported to the B-17 bomber aircraft to which we were assigned, proceeded to set up and load our guns with rounds of ammunition, and checked the operation of the solenoid switches to ensure they would fire.

At 5:00 a.m., a few hours after my enlisted crew had reported to the B-17, the officers—the pilot, co-pilot, navigator, and bombardier—arrived and performed a pre-flight check. We would be a total of nine on this mission instead of the usual ten. My crew and I didn't know any of the officers, who were already dressed in their full flight gear. Each of us piled our personal equipment—including parachutes and K-rations—inside, and packed the resist section of the plane with armor plating to protect us from anti-aircraft fire.

When the entire Eighth Air Force was flying on any particular day, it took nearly two hours for each group to assemble and get into formation prior to crossing the English Channel. Take-off was sometime in the morning. I don't recall the exact time we crossed the English Channel and hit the French coast, but we started receiving flak (anti-aircraft fire) as soon as we approached France.

It was almost two months after D-Day; the Allied forces had secured only the Cherbourg Peninsula, located in the northwest corner of France, and a small area of the French coast near Caen. As we were approaching the target, one of the guys—either Church or Panasuk—alerted us to a fire in the bomb bay. Since I was tucked into the ball turret, this wasn't the most comforting news to hear.

After what seemed like hours, though it was only seconds, I heard someone say, "Let Davis out of the ball." They could have saved their breath, because I already had the guns pointed down and the turret locked, ready to get out of the ball as quickly as I could. I was helped out of the turret, then walked along a six-inch wide catwalk to the bomb bay, which was open. We were at 25,000 feet and I still didn't have my parachute on. The crew handed me seven or eight fire extinguishers, and I tried my best to put out the fire—but attempts were futile. I'm certain my youth played a big part in my not panicking because we were carrying twenty 250-pound high-exploding bombs. I suppose if I had been older, I would have gone ape.

When it was apparent we were fighting a losing battle with the fire, we were ordered to abandon ship. At about this time, or maybe before the red light came on to abandon ship, the pilot—who was flying with our crew for the first time—entered the bomb bay with his parachute on and jumped. I later learned he was captured by the Germans and became a POW. We all made a dash for the nearest door, when fortunately I looked down and noticed that the ripcord of my parachute was on the left side when it was supposed to be on the right. I had put my parachute on backward! I nearly panicked, but managed to get it off, and put it on properly. I was the next one out of the ship after the pilot.

I thought back to gunnery school and was grateful that I had paid attention in parachute training class. We'd been taught to delay pulling the cord for three reasons: to get away from enemy fighters in the area, to avoid the extreme cold, and to descend low enough where the oxygen is plentiful enough to breathe. In falling, it seemed as if I were lying down with several large fans blowing on me. I fell and fell, wondering if I had delayed long enough—there's always a feeling of wanting to pull the ripcord immediately. I soon entered a cloud, couldn't see the ground, and decided it was time to pull the ripcord. I gave it a yank, and it sounded like a rifle shot. My legs felt as if they were being jerked off.

When the chute opened it felt as if I was going back up. "I'm not heavy enough to pull this chute down," I said to myself. I looked down. The ground was getting closer, and I saw that I was drifting toward a small town, which must have been Fontenay, France. In school they taught us how to control our flight in the parachute by pulling and flipping the lines. I started flipping like crazy, and to my pleasant surprise, I started moving away from the town.

"I get another 'A' for paying attention in class," I thought to myself. The ground was coming up rapidly, and I prepared myself for landing as I'd been trained: legs bent, pull, shroud lines at the last minute to ease landing, etc. I hit the ground stiff-legged and was jarred from head to toe. As the chute's billowy canopy made landfall, I jumped over it so I wouldn't be dragged behind it along the ground.

I took a few moments to gather my wits after my surprisingly uneventful landing. I'd landed in a wheat field, and later learned it was outside the town of Fontenay, about twenty miles north of Paris. There were workers in the field, and they yelled to me.

"Are you American?" they asked.

"Yes," I assured them as they ran over to me, and took my flying jacket, flight suit, and boots. They even wanted my parachute (which was made of silk), but I managed to secure a section of it. And then they disappeared. A little later, two Germans on motorcycles came searching for me; they were only about twelve feet away, but the Good Lord was with me: I remained undetected in the wheat field—in my underwear—with only my escape kit, wrist watch, and the crocheted baby bootie my wife Jerry had made when she was pregnant [with our daughter Jackie] and given to me when I left for England. Jackie was less than four weeks old when I was shot down. Around 10:00 p.m., Eugene Phalempin came to my aid. Eugene was a French corporal who was serving with the French Underground. He brought

me clothing and shoes that, to my surprise, fit perfectly. With a rake in hand to complete my disguise, I followed Eugene into town where we stopped at a house to eat. Because I hadn't eaten in many hours, I was famished. We'd no sooner sat down at the table when the door flew open, and some French men shouted something (in French, of course) that I didn't understand. I know now they were saying that a German patrol was coming. Before I knew what was happening, I was given a black robe, similar to a poncho, but with only a hole for my head—no arm holes. They hustled Eugene and me out the door and on to bicycles. They didn't bother to ask if I could ride a bike!

My future was in Eugene's hands. We pedaled for hours, and I had no idea where we were going. At several road crossings, we passed German soldiers. We pushed on and finally arrived at Eugene and his wife's home in Paris. Madame Phalempin prepared breakfast for us, and I finally got to eat. Then I had the most relaxing nap.

After sunrise Eugene told me we were going someplace else, but we'd have to make a stop on the way. We mounted our bicycles and started through Paris. At one point, Eugene was almost hit by a speeding car. It scared the daylights out of me. I don't know what I would have done if he had been hit: I had no idea how to get back to his home or where we were going. Our first stop was a house on a very busy street near the Arc de Triomphe. We parked our bicycles and entered. I was introduced to a man who I later learned was from British Intelligence. (Germans sometimes tried to infiltrate the underground chain by posing as downed Allied airmen, so I had to prove I was who I claimed to be.) For two or three hours, I was questioned incessantly by the man and his colleagues. They asked simple questions such as "Where did you go to school?" and "Who is your family doctor?" They had no idea if my answers were correct, but they wanted to see how quickly I responded.

"What does the number 598 mean to you?" one gentleman asked.

I shook my head, unable to think.

"What was the number of your B-17?" he then asked.

And then I remembered ... 598 were the last three numbers of our aircraft. One of the men told me the plane hadn't exploded on impact, but had disintegrated during the fall and had landed several miles north of Paris. I thought that statement was probably true since the bombardier had released the bombs we carried over open farm land outside of Paris prior to bailing out.

Eugene and I stayed in the house for two nights, and the night before we left, a funny thing happened. A group came in to my room, and we played some kind of card game. It wasn't long before I needed a drink of water, but I didn't know how to ask. So I picked up a bottle on the table and, thinking it was water, I filled a glass to the brim. Everyone began to laugh—and I soon found out why. The bottle I'd thought contained water turned out to be a strong gin.

When Eugene and I were released, we set out once again on our bicycles. I had to take all of this on faith not knowing the future. This time we rode for quite a while, and soon we arrived at the Hospital of Paris (La Salpetriere). The hospital was in two large sections with driveways in the middle. The French utilized one side, and the Germans the other side. I later found out that my crewmate Waterfield had broken his leg when he landed, was captured, and was on the German side of the hospital. I was escorted inside the hospital and put under the care of Marie Laure, a member of the French underground chain. I was to spend a couple of days there until I was normal again.

Marie Laure spoke English, and it was such a relief to talk to someone who could understand me. She asked if I needed anything—some food, or perhaps something to read.

"I'd enjoy having something to read," I told her.

She left, and soon after a young boy appeared with a copy of the "Lord Earth."

My first full day in the hospital, I told Marie Laure about my daughter whom I hadn't yet seen, as she was born the day I flew my 23rd mission, July 11, 1944. I asked Marie Laure if she could somehow get a small gift I could take home to her. (My faith grew stronger each minute that I would get home.) I still had my escape kit which contained forty-eight French francs. I handed her the francs and asked that she use her own judgment to select a gift. She purchased a necklace: a chain with a small cross. I now had two possessions I was determined to carry home for my daughter: the necklace and the baby bootie, which I'd tied to the shoulder strap of my flight jacket and had carried on every mission.

Marie Laure and I were enjoying a card game when there was a knock at the door. A slip of paper was shoved underneath, which indicated we were to leave at six o'clock the next morning. It was now the 5th or 6th of August. Eugene and I mounted our bicycles at the designated time, and travelled to the metropolitan subway station. Eugene had a backpack, so I figured we were going to do a little walking. But I was wrong: once we arrived at the station, we boarded the railway. I was really concerned when we entered the railway car because there were German soldiers all over the place. Many of them were German officers in civilian clothes who were fleeing Paris. Eugene and I became separated and when people boarded the train, he kept getting shoved toward the front while I was wedged in the back.

Thank goodness the backpack stuck out in the crowd so I could keep track of Eugene. Several times German soldiers looked right at me. I made myself stare straight ahead. You can imagine the thoughts going through my mind. I was told to say nothing, and to act deaf and dumb. This was not hard to do. I was terrified I'd give myself away.

We finally arrived at the end of the line. I waited until Eugene got off and then followed him. We remained at the station for what seemed hours, and I wasn't sure exactly what we were waiting for. Finally a truck pulled up and I was told to get aboard. There were French men, women, and children on the truck who were going to work in some big factories. These were, I suppose, similar to our American factory workers. We travelled on the truck until we arrived at our destination.

I had mixed emotions: I was sad to say farewell to Eugene, who'd been with me since I was picked up in the wheat field and gotten me this far. Yet, it was a happy moment because I was this much closer to home—and freedom. I could feel it. Freedom.

Our destination was the town of Rambouillet, where I was taken to the home of Madame Christiane Le Febvre.[9]

---

[9] Sincere thanks to Jimmy C. Davis, son of Jack Davis, for permission to include his father's personal account in this book. Davis received a Purple Heart, Distinguished Flying Cross, and an Air Medal with four oak-leaf clusters in WWII. He received a Purple Heart, which regretfully was not placed on his record, in the Korean War. Colonel Davis passed away in 1989.

Top Secret.

TOP SECRET.
I.S.9 (WEA)

APPENDIX " C " TO E. & E. REPORT No. 189(WEA)/6/154 /514

If further circulation of this information is made, it is important that its source should not be divulged.

No. 18168685   Rank. S/Sgt   Name Jack C. Davis

Date of Interview.   22 August 1944

Mlle Marie Laude, Hopital Salpetriere, Paris kept the
narrator for 2 days.

M. et Mme. Claude le Febvre, 44 Rue du Petit Parc, Rambouillet,
Seine et Marne kept the narrator and 5 other evaders for 2 weeks.

M. Prompsand (member of Resistance) 2 Rue Dubru, Rambouillet
brought them news and helped in small ways.

Top Secret.

Official Debrief EE-1128 JDavis (Declassified file)

CHAPTER SIX

FOR THE SAKE OF MY SON

In the meantime my life was still a little bit messy and *bordélique*, but it was a very happy mess. I quit my job and began working as an independent perfumer, which gave me a lot of freedom—and then I discovered I was pregnant. I wanted to stay relatively close to family so my yet-unborn child would be able to form connections with relatives; but, I knew that to have a successful perfume business, it would be beneficial to live in a large, international city. Sascha and I considered moving to London, Rome, and Berlin. As it turned out, the answer became obvious: we visited Berlin and fell in love with the city for its quality of life and green space. Since German is his first language, Sascha was thrilled. I did impose one condition, however: I needed to have a little *pied-à-terre* in my dear Paris. It took well over a year to find our special little place in Paris and renovate it. During that time, our baby boy was born, and we named him Carl after Sascha's Austrian father. Finally, in late April 2013, we moved in with our little Carl, who was already ten months old.

Carl watched with curious eyes from his little bassinette on the floor while Sascha and I unpacked box after box of our possessions.

Then I opened the box containing two important files: the one in which I had placed Amy's letter and the one Maman had given me nearly two years earlier.

"Did you ever hear back from your Uncle Patrice?" Sascha asked as I removed the file from the carton.

"No," I said, and it suddenly dawned on me how quickly time had passed.

It's strange how parenthood changes a person's perspective. I thought about all the years I was oblivious of an important chapter in my ancestors' lives and how the file in my hand contained not only a piece of my family history, but also that of my darling son's. Then and there, I resolved that Carl would know the truth about his family's past. He'd grow up aware of his heritage—both French and Austrian. In order to accomplish this, I knew I'd have to further investigate the story of Grand-père Claude and his mother, Christiane. I still wondered if my great-grandmother had broken the law ... the thought put a bitter taste in my mouth. *If she did do something wrong, I wasn't ready to hear it two years ago, but now I am. I'm prepared to discover the truth.*

My first thought was that I must get in contact with the American, Amy Schmidt, who had written the letter to Papa and Maman. But how would I reach her? She seemed to be of my parents' generation, and since my papa had passed away at such a young age—he was only forty-four—I knew there was always the terrible possibility that Amy may have passed as well. I considered sending her a letter via the postal service, but that method would take too long.

Resolutely, I opened my laptop and Googled "Amy Schmidt."

CHAPTER SEVEN

SEARCHING FOR AMY
Paris—April, 2013

My Google search for Amy Schmidt yielded nothing. However, the stubborn side of me wasn't willing to give up so quickly, and I decided to try another approach: Facebook. Several people named Amy Schmidt popped up when I typed in the name. I looked again at the return address on the envelope Amy had sent nearly three years earlier to remind myself of her hometown, and then quickly scanned the Facebook results one more time, and ... there was an Amy Schmidt in Peachtree City, Georgia! *This has to be the Amy Schmidt I'm looking for!* My fingers flew over the keyboard as I messaged her.

> *Dear Amy,*
>
> *I don't know if you're the Amy Cotts Schmidt I'm looking for. My name is Marie Le Febvre. I am Didier's daughter to whom, if you are the right person, you sent a letter three years ago after the death of your father. If you are this person, I want to thank you and I really would love to exchange with you.*
>
> *Many thanks for your answer.*

Marie (Paris, France)

I took a deep breath, hit "enter," and waited.

It was the 20th of April when I messaged Amy and, of course, I had hoped to hear back from her right away. I checked my Facebook account repeatedly over the next couple of days, and was extremely disappointed when I received no reply. The more hours that passed without hearing from her, the more I dwelt on possible reasons why Amy hadn't responded. *Had I waited too long to contact her? Perhaps she has no interest in corresponding, or maybe she's ill and unable to answer.* Then another thought struck me. *Amy's probably the same age as my mother, and like Maman, she may not visit her Facebook page all that often. What if Amy only goes on Facebook once every few months?* If this was the case, I knew I couldn't just sit around waiting for a reply. So I went back to Amy's Facebook page and read through her profile. I noted she had a son, Peter, and searched to see if he, too, had a Facebook profile—which he did. I sent Peter a brief message explaining who I was, and that I had messaged his mother. I asked if he would tell her to look on Facebook. And then I anxiously waited some more.

On April 26, 2013, Amy messaged back.

Hello Marie.

I am the person who sent you the letter after the death of my dad. Without your brave family, I would not be here today. Thank you! I would love to exchange with you.

Amy

And with those words, my ancestors' story began to unravel.

CHAPTER EIGHT

FROM ACROSS THE ATLANTIC

Paris, France and Peachtree City, Georgia, U.S.—May 2013

Whyhen I heard back from Amy, I was overjoyed—and more resolved than ever to search for answers. I immediately messaged Amy on Facebook thanking her for the letter to my parents,
and telling her that Papa had passed away in 1996. I also asked if
she would share what she knew of my great-grandparents and Grand-
père Claude. Two days later, she messaged me back.

Dear Marie,

*I didn't know your father had passed away. I'm so sorry for
your loss.*

*I'm happy to share the story of how my Dad met your family,
along with some other details. But before I do, I want you to know
I've been told that your great-grandparents and grandparents
were incredibly courageous people. You must be very proud to be
a member of such a brave family. My dad was told your Great-
grandfather Georges had been arrested by the Nazis, and spent
the war in a prisoner camp in Germany, so my dad never met him.*

My dad was a co-pilot of a B-17 aircraft called Moonglow, which was shot down during a bombing mission. The Germans were watching, and so was the French Resistance. They used to count the number of men who bailed, watch where they landed, and then look for them. The pilot was taken prisoner of war, and some of the crew were killed. My dad made contact with the French Resistance and eventually was passed along to your Great-grandmother Christiane in Rambouillet, where he met other airmen. It was there he met up with two members of his crew: the navigator and the bombardier. They had been found by the French Resistance. An American fighter pilot was also with them.

Your great-grandmother took care of these men, and my father adored her for it. She treated him like her own children. She was kind, generous, and thoughtful. Everyone understood if the Nazis found out what she did, she would be shot. My dad said she helped seventeen airmen of various nationalities during the war. Your Grandfather Claude received the Battle Cross with two silver stars in a ceremony at the town square in Rambouillet. I have a picture! He and my dad were close in age and became fast friends. Your grandfather was a Resistance fighter, and my dad said that during his stay at Christiane's, your grandfather used to come and go with other men—but my dad didn't know where they were going or what they were doing.

My parents visited your grandfather in the 1980s. During that visit, your grandfather revealed a bit more of his own story: When he was coming and going from Christiane's, he cooperated with a small group of Resistance fighters, joining them in trying to frustrate the Germans through surprise attacks. This group used to go building by building and room by room to make their surprise attacks. In one instance, they came up behind a German sniper who heard them. He was killed, but not before whipping around and spraying the group with machine gun fire. Your grandfather was hit and sustained a serious injury.

My father also met your Grandmother Jeannine. I don't know much about her other than that she understood what was going on in your great-grandparents' home, and was loyal to them and your grandfather.

If you have more information on your family, I would love to hear what you have found.

May I please have your email address? I have a few letters I would like to copy and send to you.

Best Regards,

Amy

I was speechless.

CHAPTER NINE

OPENING THE PAST
Paris, France—May 2013

I sat for a few minutes trying to process this new information. I was stunned. How bizarre to learn all this from a person I really didn't know. If Amy had more information, I was eager to know more.

After collecting my thoughts, I sent Amy my email address, and told her about the half-note from the French Underground member who'd claimed my great-grandmother had never received recognition from the French government. I asked her if she had any idea why Great-Grandmother Christiane wouldn't be acknowledged by her own country for her role during the war, and, more precisely, if she knew whether my great-grandmother had done something wrong.

I wondered what kind of documents Amy wanted to send to me. I was overjoyed with the opportunity to connect with Amy, and extremely grateful she'd been able to tell me so much about Grand-père's wartime experiences. If only she'd be able to shed some light on the question of the half-note and why my great-grandmother's contributions during the war weren't formally recognized by her own government. That information would have been the icing on the cake for me. Amy's response was sympathetic, but unfortunately she didn't have an answer.

Dear Marie,

Unfortunately, I have no idea why your great-grandmother wasn't honored by France. She was very brave. I have two sons, eighteen and twenty-one years old. I imagine they are the same age as the airmen Christiane took into her home. They were complete strangers, and she provided them with a safe haven and a refuge from fear; she mothered them with loving hospitality. I can only imagine the silent fears that lived in her heart for her husband, for her son, and the fear she might be betrayed at any minute. She did not know what the outcome would be. She sacrificed for a future she might not see or be able to enjoy.

While my dad was there, the [Rambouillet] train station was bombed by the Eighth Air Force.[10] I imagine your great-grandmother knew it would be years after the war before all could be rebuilt, and she had to know her life would not be as it was before the war. She should have gotten a medal for her sacrifices, and I'm surprised she didn't. Obviously, there were many who felt strongly she deserved the medal.

I have copies of letters to send you, but please be patient as it may take a few days.

Kind regards,

Amy

I had no idea what Amy would be sending me. I assumed it would be a few documents, and welcomed any information she could share—anything that would help me put the pieces of this puzzle together.

---

10   Historical records indicate that the Ninth Air Force bombed the Rambouillet train station.

A few days later, I received another email from Amy. She told me that the next day, Sunday, May 12th, was Mother's Day in the United States. "From one mother to another," she wrote, "this is my gift to you!" Her message was followed by email after email, each with several documents attached—twenty emails and fifty attachments in all. I was floored. That was the night the ground fell away beneath me.

With little Carl sound asleep and Sascha on a business trip in London, our flat was quiet. I made a pot of coffee, and settled myself on the sofa with my laptop. As I read each document, I was drawn deeper and deeper into a mesmerizing story. But these documents recounted more than just a story—they detailed the lives and actions of real people—and at that point, WWII became very real to me. There was information about Amy's father, Russell Cotts. His story helped me understand what it meant to be an American officer during the war, and how it felt to be shot down and escape capture by the Germans. And, there was Jack Davis' account, which really hit home with me: I learned that not only was Great-grandmother Christiane involved in the Underground, so was Grand-père Claude.

Thanks to Amy, I knew that Grand-père à Chapeau had been taken captive by the Germans during the war. There was a letter telling of his return from the German POW camp where he'd been held prisoner for more than four years. Several emails later, I received a description of the camps, and I could feel my grandmother's horror deep in the pit of my stomach. The account was so difficult to read, I found myself gasping for air. I couldn't take it all in. In addition to letters, Amy had sent some pictures: the house in Rambouillet, and faded photos of Christiane and Claude. And, for the very first time, I saw Christiane's photo and read her handwriting. Just a couple short years earlier, I'd never even heard my great-grandmother's name; but, there she was, looking back at me and inviting me not only into an account of WWII, but into my family's past.

Then I opened a document that contained information about Grand-père Claude, and the contents caught me completely off guard: There was a brief passage indicating he hoped to become a military pilot. *A pilot?* I was stunned. *Grand-père never mentioned this to me. I'm his granddaughter, and I thought I knew him so well. We spent many hours together, yet I had no idea he wanted to fly!* I was disappointed he hadn't shared his ambition with me, but at the same time—and for a very special reason—I felt an even closer bond with my grandfather.

No one in my family had ever mentioned wanting to become a pilot, but I'd privately fantasized about flying for many years. When I finally decided to turn my dream into reality and earned my pilot's license, I kept my accomplishment a secret for quite some time before mentioning it to anyone. And, it would be several years before I discovered that I'd learned to fly over the exact same land where Jack Davis and Russell Cotts had abandoned their aircraft and found safety in my great-grandmother's home.

I developed a love of travel early in life, and have been lucky enough to explore many countries with my family and friends. I've always been passionate about discovering new places and experiencing unique colors, lights, smells, tastes, histories, and cultures. And I'm positive these adventures influenced my creativity and inspiration as a perfumer. But my secret passion is to fly—to touch the sky—to float among the clouds and look down on the earth from above. Flying gives me such an incredible feeling of freedom and humility.

I attended flight school when I was thirty with this clear-cut purpose in mind. Although I lacked confidence and was unsure if I could pass the exam, I was driven to prove I could do it. And I did. I worked hard and succeeded. In addition to learning that flying requires discipline, practice, rigor, and trust in others, I discovered a great deal about myself and my abilities. It's difficult to describe the sense of accomplishment I felt, but it's even harder to describe how exhilarating it feels to take off, to touch the sky, to land! I've also visited some of the most amazing places and enjoyed incredible experiences, including flying over and visiting lands that are worlds apart from my own, and participating in competitions like the Breitling 100/24 Cup, which challenges crews to take off and land at one hundred airports throughout France during a twenty-four-hour period.

But perhaps what has touched me most about being a pilot is being able to fly in the same skies as the pilots whose stories I've discovered. Although I never met Jack Davis or Russell Cotts, I feel a sense of connection to them as I've soared in the same airspace in which they encountered German fire. Thanks to my flying experience, coupled with an active imagination, I can nearly picture the horrific situations in which they found themselves: forced to keep a cool head in order to survive when their plane has been shot and the engine is burning, and not knowing whether the Germans would be waiting when they touched the ground. And, I wonder, *What would have I done in their situation? Would I have been as brave as those young airmen?*

But most of all, I became part of a new family—the flying family. This isn't something I was expecting, and I was grateful to be able to take advantage of the special ties among those of us who fly. I was a new pilot when Sascha received a call from Austria late one Sunday afternoon. It was not good news: His father, who was nearly ninety, had been rushed to the hospital and had only hours left to live. There was no way Sascha could get there on time by taking a commercial flight, and I didn't yet have my instrument rating, which meant I couldn't pilot the plane by myself. I quickly dialled Patrick, my dear friend and flight instructor.

"Patrick, we have an emergency. Sascha's dad has been rushed to the hospital and has only hours to live. Can we make a flight to Klagenfurt?" I asked.

"Unfortunately, I'm in Germany, on my way home from a flying expo," Patrick replied. "Why don't you call Jacques?"

I'd flown with Jacques only a couple of times before, but I phoned him and explained the situation.

"I'm so sorry, I really can't," he said. "I'll call you back in fifteen minutes."

Sascha and I waited nervously by the phone, and I grabbed it on the first ring less than ten minutes later.

"Gilles is expecting you at Toussus-Le-Noble airfield in forty-five minutes. I don't think you know Gilles, but he'll fly you to Austria. You can drop off Sascha and make the return flight with Gilles. It's a long flight, so you'll assist Gilles on the way back."

Just before takeoff, we learned that Sascha's dad had passed, but we were able to get Sascha to Austria within a few hours. I will never be able to thank my fellow pilots for what they did. I call them my *chevaliers du ciel* (knights in the sky). The return flight was one I'll always remember: A full moon reflected the most beautiful light over the Alps on a crystal-clear night. The scene was incredibly intense. Around five o'clock in the morning, Gilles and I landed back at Le Bourget, the only Paris airport open twenty-four hours. I thanked Gilles from the bottom of my heart, and felt so proud to be part of the flying family. Aviators share a special bond as every aspect of flying is based in trust, solidarity and cooperation.

I'll always delight in the kinship I share with my flying family, and I'm strongly convinced my grandfather somehow inspired me to take those bold steps toward becoming a part of that community. Without realizing it, when I got my license, I'd also honored his memory and his ambitions. Perhaps I'm more like my grandfather than I thought. After all, we're both Le Febvres, and his blood runs through my veins. No matter what, I'm certain Grand-père Claude would be proud to know I've accomplished a goal that was dear to him. I also feel a sense of connection to the American airmen whose lives were saved by my family during the war.

Late into the night, as I was about to open another document, it dawned on me that Grand-père's birthday was the 13th of July. I'd been so busy, I'd completely forgotten his birth date. Carl was born on July 12th, just a few minutes before midnight. This thought completely overwhelmed me. I'd held back the deluge of tears until that moment, but could no longer stem the flow.

I walked slowly and silently into Carl's bedroom, lifted him from his tiny bed, and cuddled him for a few minutes as I stared into his beautiful face. He was still sound asleep when I put him back in his crib, my tears dripping on his little pajamas. I went back to the sofa and continued my *nuit blanche,* (all-nighter). It was just as well that Sascha was away because I wouldn't have been able to speak, not with him, not with anyone. The more I read, the more I cried.

The next day, I knew exactly what I needed to do—fly. So up into the skies I went. French flight regulations prevented me from flying directly over Rambouillet, so I flew around it, and soared over the area where the B-17 Moonglow had been shot down so many years before. I took a photo for Amy. The visibility wasn't that great and neither was the photo, but it was something I just had to do.

CHAPTER TEN

ANOTHER AIRMAN'S TALE

landed the plane, but my mind was still soaring as I continued to soak in the information I'd received from Amy, including her account of her father's last mission. Below is the first half of this story.

The Long Walk Back

My dad's story always was a part of the fabric of our family. Although he rarely initiated a conversation about what he experienced during the war, he did talk about it when prompted, usually by my mother. I was very young when I first learned the details and didn't always understand the significance of the events he described, but I remember feeling fascinated by the account and being proud of his accomplishments.

My father co-piloted a B-17 during the war. Unlike fighter planes, which engaged enemy fighter planes in direct warfare (called dog fights), B-17s were bombers. Waist gunners and ball turret gunners were on board to combat enemy attacks, but these planes carried heavy bombs and weren't at all agile in the air. Fighter planes accompanied B-17s on their missions for additional protection, but they couldn't carry enough fuel to escort the bombers the entire way since fighter aircraft needed to be light enough to maneuver in battle.

At the tender age of twenty, Dad was assigned one final mission as co-pilot before he would be placed in charge of piloting his own crew. There was something different about this mission: The officers and the crew had never flown together before. My dad said that made the mission even more dangerous because if the plane was shot down, members of the French Resistance might think the crew members were German spies since they couldn't respond to simple questions about each other.

"The target of this bombing mission was a synthetic oil refinery in Saint Germain-en-Laye near Paris," my dad told us.

As the bombers approached the target area, they were hit with heavy anti-aircraft fire. "Flak struck the plane," said Dad, "and it immediately filled with smoke. A fire had started in the left wing and spread into the bomb bay. Our B-17 quickly slid out of formation, and the pilot ordered the bombardier to salvo the bombs to prevent an explosion." The pilot, a veteran of thirty-two missions, jumped from his seat to help put out the fire and left my dad to fly the aircraft. That was quite a challenge: The plane had lost its two left engines.

The rest of the bombing group had continued on to the primary target, so the crew on the damaged aircraft was alone in the air, and vulnerable to enemy fighter planes. The scene was chaotic as they tried to extinguish the fire, and the plane's propeller faltered. At one point, the pilot passed out from lack of oxygen; the navigator managed to revive the pilot, who then went to the back of the plane to check on the other crew members. My dad had his hands full trying to hold the aircraft level while the navigator plotted a course back to England avoiding known flak areas in France from the aerial maps on board. But as the plane *steadily lost altitude, it was doubtful the crew would ever make it back across the English Channel.*

At this point, smoke was billowing through the plane, and the pilot hadn't returned to his seat, so my dad radioed the bombardier to go to the back of the plane and check on the other crew members. After a quick tour of the interior, the bombardier reported that everyone who'd been in the back of the plane had bailed out—including the pilot—which left only him, the navigator, and my dad on board the aircraft. My dad ordered the other two men to escape through the open bomb bay. Then he set the trim tabs to hold the plane as level as possible and followed them, stepping out of the plane through the bomb bay doors.

Dad's downward descent was frightening. "I plummeted through the air on my back and delayed opening my parachute for as long as possible to avoid being visible to the enemy," he later said. "Out of the corner of my eye, I saw the airplane about a quarter of a mile away and slightly above me as it headed into a steep spiral and erupted in a huge explosion. The bomber disintegrated into a pile of flames, smoke, and burning debris as it fell to earth."

Flipping over as the ground rushed up at him, my father pulled the ripcord, and the parachute billowed open. He discovered he was coming down over a lake flanked on one side by a recreation area or resort. Dozens of people in unmistakable attire— the green uniform of German soldiers—were visible below.

Dad said, "I worried that my heavy boots would weigh me down if I landed in the lake, so I tried to kick them off as I descended— an impossible task." As luck would have it, however, instead of floating straight down, the chute began to drift to the left of the water and eventually fell into a wooded area. Just like in the movies, Dad ended up suspended in the branches of a tree, and he was left dangling ten or fifteen feet above ground. He tugged and tugged on the lines before the branches finally gave way, and he fell to the ground below.

According to his watch, it was now 5:30 p.m. Dad pulled his chute together, rolled the fabric and cords into a ball, and hid the bundle beneath some leaves. A country road ran through the woods, and he could hear people and vehicles in the distance. Afraid he'd be discovered by the enemy, my dad hid in a nearby ditch.

An hour later, two young French children walked down the lane toting baskets of nuts they'd picked in the woods. My dad had his escape kit with him: a French-English dictionary, maps, French currency, and a few other items. He approached the children and used the dictionary to indicate that he was an American and needed help. The children pointed to his watch, letting him know that they'd return later and left. Once again, my dad hid, but this time in a different place. He wasn't completely certain he could trust the children, and didn't want to be in the same location as before in case they came back with Germans.

But the children were as good as their word. Two French civilians, members of the Underground, approached several hours later. They took my dad to a small isolated shed in the countryside and helped him climb into the attic. Handing him a bottle of wine and a loaf of black bread, they told him to stay put for the night.

As morning dawned, numerous German ME-109 planes took off directly over the shed. Dad distinctly remembered the rumble of the planes and their low flight overhead. "I recall thinking I could reach out and touch them," he said.

His rescuers returned later that morning with a civilian suit and shoes. After my dad changed, they disposed of his uniform, and together they started walking along the back roads. Dad was then passed along from one underground cell to another. He wasn't exactly sure where he was going, but he had to trust that these brave people were leading him to safety.

As it turned out, he was headed for the town of Rambouillet and the home of Madame Christiane Le Febvre.[11]

---

11 Sincere thanks to Amy Cotts Schmidt, daughter of Russell Cotts, for contributing this story, which is partially excerpted from a paper written by Amy's mother for a college English class. Russell Cotts was awarded the Distinguished Flying Cross. He retired from the Air Force a as a Lieutenant Colonel. Russell Cotts passed away in 2009.

CHAPTER ELEVEN

RESISTING FOR FREEDOM

Amy was right about my great-grandmother Christiane: She was, indeed, a brave woman. As I write this book, it's been two years since my initial Facebook exchanges with Amy. The numerous documents she sent me fueled my desire to learn more about my ancestors' role in the war. Before receiving them, WWII wasn't on my radar; and, until these documents opened my eyes to the roles Christiane and Grand-père played, I honestly didn't care about this chapter in my country's history. But, thanks to Amy, I've developed a passion for learning about the past.

In addition to discovering and reading a book about the liberation of Rambouillet, I've contacted the French military, the French Resistance Association, and the newspaper *Toutes Les Nouvelles*, and followed as many leads as possible. Amy also provided me with the names of two French gentlemen with whom her dad had been in touch in 2003. I attempted to make contact with both of them, but one of them had passed away. However, I've met several times with Monsieur Didier Cornevin. His passion is studying planes that were shot down in and around Paris during WWII, and he generously shared documents and records that helped me better understand how the French Resistance operated, and my great-grandmother's part in it.

Christiane was only fifteen years old at the outset of World War I, and nineteen years old when the war ended. Four years later, she married Georges Le Febvre (Grand-père à Chapeau), who'd proudly defended his country during WWI and was decorated with France's highest Medal of Honor: the *Chevalier de la Legion d'Honneur.* He also served in WWII, but was captured by the Germans early on, and remained a prisoner of war until the Liberation.

At the dawn of WWII, French women maintained traditional roles. They didn't have the right to vote, and couldn't even open a bank account without the consent of a husband or father. But during the war, women had to step into the shoes of their husbands, brothers, fathers, and sons, just as their mothers did when their men fought during WWI. Like their female counterparts in the United States who were supporting the war effort by working in factories, French women provided for their families, and some contributed to the fight for their country's freedom by joining the Resistance. That's what my great-grandmother Christiane did when she was contacted by a member of the local Underground.

The French Resistance

Perhaps you have run across references to the French Underground, the Resistance, Resistance Fighters, Freedom Fighters, or similar terms in books and movies. In school, we French aren't taught much about World War II, other than the fact that we won. So, a movie provided my first real exposure to these brave individuals. Produced in the 1970s, "La Grande Vadrouille" ("The Great Stroll") is a comedy about two Frenchmen helping the crew of a Royal Air Force bomber escape arrest during the German occupation. Whatever label they're given, these men and women were all part of the French Resistance, and they shared a common goal: to fight for their country's freedom.

In school we had been taught that Charles de Gaulle was the head of the Resistance, but as I investigated this movement I found we had only learned part of the story. French historian Henry Russo coined the term "French Resistancialism myth" in 1987[12] to describe fabrications created by Gaullists and Communists that have generated misconceptions. He points out that almost all French citizens were résistants from the beginning of the war. Of course, during my school days we were taught that almost every French man, woman, and child was a résistant during the war, and that de Gaulle was a superhero who liberated France entirely on his own—well, perhaps with only the tiniest bit of help from the Allies. And, yes, there were a small number of individuals who weren't good people—the Collabos. But doesn't every country have a few rotten apples? Unfortunately, these stereotypes—and the feelings they've produced—still exist today. I'm not trying to minimize the role played by de Gaulle and the résistants during WWII. However, we French should not forget all the Allies who supported the Resistance: Without their extraordinary courage and commitment to freedom, my mother tongue could well have been German.

Résistants represented every layer of society: doctors and peasants, housewives (like my great-grandmother) and telephone operators, farmers and postal workers, young and old—they were ordinary people who, until the war, lived ordinary lives. Under German occupation, however, these same people became saboteurs, spies, rescuers, and fighters. After Pétain signed the armistice with Germany in June 1940, some French were relieved that there would be no more war. Many were still reeling from the trauma they'd suffered during WWI, and thought that the Armistice provided insurance against further death and destruction. Some supporters also reasoned that the Third Reich would protect France from the threat of Communism as the Soviet Union expanded. But of course, they had no idea what their future would hold under the Nazis. Others, however, were appalled by the prospect of surrendering to the Germans; they opposed Nazism and everything it stood for, and they began to take matters into their own hands.

---

12 Rousso, Henry. (1987). *Le Syndrome de Vichy: de 1944 à nos jours.* Paris: Editions du Seuil.

During the early days of WWII, de Gaulle was a colonel in the French army. He spearheaded two successful attacks against the Germans in May 1940, which resulted in their retreat. In fact, de Gaulle was the only French commander to halt Germany's advance during their invasion of France, and his actions were rewarded with a promotion to provisional brigadier general. Like several of his compatriots, de Gaulle steadfastly opposed the Nazis, and he was horrified when government leaders agreed to an armistice. Rather than suffer the humiliation of surrender, he went to London where he requested permission to broadcast to the French via the BBC. The British cabinet denied his request, but British Prime Minister Winston Churchill overruled their decision. On June 18, 1940, de Gaulle, who was virtually unknown in France at that time, delivered what would become his most famous radio broadcast. His words delivered inspiration and hope to his fellow countrymen.

> *Has the last word been spoken? Must all hope be gone? Is defeat definitive? No! Believe me ... when I tell you that nothing is lost for France ... and we are not alone. The vast British Empire is behind us and like the British, we can avail ourselves of the immense industry of the United States. This war is not limited to France—it is a world war. I invite French officers and soldiers who are in Britain with or without their arms, and I invite engineers and skilled armament workers who are on British soil, or who have the means to come here, to join me. The flame of the French Resistance must not and will not be extinguished.*[13]

De Gaulle's message encouraged his compatriots to continue their fight against Nazism under his leadership and marked the beginning of the Free French movement. He continued to urge his fellow citizens to resist via the rousing five-minute messages he delivered as part of a half-hour news program broadcast in French by the BBC. Each evening, these broadcasts served as motivators for many French citizens and kept them positively focused on their goal: freedom.

---

13 Charles de Gaulle Foundation. Appel du 18 Juin 1940 du Général de Gaulle. Retrieved from http://charles-de-gaulle.org. Williams, Michael. Oradour-sur-Glane 10th June 1944. March 2000-May 2015. Retrieved from http://www.oradour.info

Meanwhile, in July 1940, Churchill authorized the creation of the Special Operations Executive (SOE). This British secret army's mission was to conduct espionage, sabotage, and reconnaissance against the Axis powers in occupied Europe, and to aid the many local resistance movements that had emerged throughout France. The Allies parachuted in arms, equipment, provisions, and other supplies to support the French underground. While the center of operations was based in England, the SOE planted undercover agents in France to help procedures run smoothly. The British government was often at odds with de Gaulle—who formed his own agency to aid Resistance workers— though they reached a compromise regarding resistance operations in the fall of 1941 and began to work together. The United States began aiding the French Resistance in 1943 as the Allied invasion of France became closer to reality: The Office of Strategic Services (OSS) began sending agents into France in cooperation with the SOE to rally French support against the German occupation.

During the first few years of its existence, the French Resistance was small, unorganized, and had no definitive command structure. It consisted of multiple cells, or resistance movements, within France. There were those that were loyal to de Gaulle (called the Free French), left-leaning groups affiliated with socialism and Communism, right-leaning groups, those that were violent and those that were not. Some cells promoted passive means of resistance, and other cells advocated violence—each group subscribed to its own philosophy and methods for achieving its goal. However, when it came to violence, few Resistance cells took more forceful action against the enemy than the *Maquis*. Notoriously brutal in their approach, the Maquisards ambushed and executed German soldiers. But no matter how different each group's beliefs and tactics, all cells were united in their desire to live in a France free of German domination. Some résistants defied the Nazis in small ways, by reading banned newspapers or listening to forbidden radio broadcasts, such as the BBC program featuring de Gaulle. Other résistants engaged in bolder actions. For example, postal workers hid and delivered Resistance mail, and even opened and photographed important German correspondence. Still others undertook aggressive measures that directly impacted the enemy, like blowing up railways or destroying telephone lines. Of course, any act of disobedience, whether subtle or brazen, was dangerous—and punishment by death was always a real threat.

Germans used propaganda as a psychological weapon during the Occupation and bombarded the French people with speeches, photographs, postcards, flyers, posters, and even art. As you've undoubtedly deduced, much of the verbal and visual indoctrination vilified Jews, but French conduct was also targeted. The Nazis tried to convince the French that their current situation was their own fault—or, if not their fault, then the war and French downfall were definitely caused by the Jews or the Communists or the British—anyone but the Germans. The résistants destroyed the propaganda as quickly as Germany produced it and launched a campaign of their own. When they tore down German posters, they put up posters supporting the Resistance effort. They also printed how-to guides for hiding from the Germans, and published Resistance newspapers.

A rallying point for the Resistance occurred three years into the Occupation when German authorities decreed that every Frenchman over the age of twenty-five would be sent to Germany for two years of labor. A dramatic surge in participation in the Resistance occurred from 1943-1944 as the numbers of résistants increased from an estimated 40,000 to 100,000. With this increase, cells became more organized, and the movement developed into a far more effective adversary of the Third Reich. Resistance members carried out more than one hundred attacks per month during the first half of 1943, and by September, the number of attacks increased fourfold. Although the attacks didn't completely stop the Germans, they did disrupt the Nazis' ability to transport supplies from one point to another.

The Resistance members' acts of courage and fight for freedom weren't without German retaliation, and in fact, German reprisal was often vicious. Captured résistants were tortured, executed, or sent to concentration camps. Innocent civilians suffered as well. One famous example is the German massacre of residents at Oradour-sur-Glane: On June 10, 1944, troops from the Waffen-SS, a paramilitary unit of the Nazi party, killed 642 townspeople—only two villagers survived—and then burned all the buildings. To this day, there is no universally accepted reason for the massacre.[14]

While General de Gaulle and the Allies were united in their fight for freedom against the Germans, they had issues among themselves: Winston Churchill and Charles de Gaulle's relationship had vacillated over the three years since June 1940, though eventually they resolved their differences and appeared to be united—until the Unites States entered the war. American President Roosevelt did not trust de Gaulle and refused to view him as a political leader; he went so far as refusing to have any discussions with him. Once France was liberated, Roosevelt planned to install a provisional Allied military government, while de Gaulle viewed himself as the future leader of France. Great Britain and the U.S. didn't share plans for D-Day with de Gaulle who was in Algiers, where he had moved his headquarters to be on French soil. (In spite of Roosevelt's disdain for de Gaulle, General Dwight D. Eisenhower, the Allied Commander-in-Chief, held the French general in high regard. While in Africa, Eisenhower assured de Gaulle that French forces—not Allied forces—would liberate Paris.) A few days before D-Day, Churchill sent two representatives to Algiers to bring de Gaulle back to Britain. Upon learning of the planned invasion, de Gaulle intended to broadcast to France on the BBC immediately after General Eisenhower, though this was not the plan of Churchill and Roosevelt. De Gaulle held his ground and ultimately won this bantam battle among the trio. Meanwhile, support for de Gaulle and the Free French was growing in France.

The French Resistance was pivotal to the success of D-Day. The Allies and Resistance had worked together since early spring to map out every detail of Operation Overlord. Their strategies came to fruition on June 5, 1944, the eve of D-Day, when the BBC broadcast 200 personal messages that signaled the résistants to activate their plans. Resistance fighters ensured railways and French communications were

---

14   Williams, Michael. *Oradour-sur-Glane 10th June 1944.* March 2000-May 2015. Retrieved from http://www.oradour.info

paralyzed within twenty-four hours, and they continued assisting Allied forces in northern and southern France after D-Day; many played key roles during the liberation of Paris on August 25. Three days after the liberation of Paris, de Gaulle appealed to all Resistance groups to disband and encouraged members to join the new French army, now under his control.

After the war, General Eisenhower acknowledged the important role the French Resistance had played when he wrote, "Throughout France the Resistance had been of inestimable value in the campaign. Without their great assistance the liberation of France would have consumed a much longer time and meant greater losses to ourselves."

I've now read countless stories detailing heroic acts by brave members of the Resistance, but those that intrigue me the most involve women. The Comet Line, of which my great-grandmother was a part, was established by a Belgian lady, Andrée De Jongh, in the spring of 1940 to help downed Allied airmen escape capture and ultimately return home to Britain. This remarkable network was comprised of 1,000 individuals throughout occupied France, neutral Spain, and England. Another noteworthy woman, French native Marie-Madeleine Fourcade, became the head of the Alliance Réseau, a Resistance network headquartered in Vichy. Madame Fourcade was captured by the Germans, and managed to escape through the window of her prison cell. She eventually joined the Maquis. These are but two examples—probably among thousands—of the incredibly brave women of the French Resistance. But the story that captivates and inspires me the most is still the tale of my own great-grandmother.

CHAPTER TWELVE

A COURAGEOUS REBEL

As I searched the archives of Office of the Resistance, I made a thrilling discovery: records and direct testimony from some of the key members, including the person who organized efforts in the Rambouillet area. And, I found statements from the man who recruited my great-grandmother!

Monsieur François Prompsaud, a stove builder, was a deeply patriotic man who became an agent for the Comet Line. A few months later he was put in charge of the entire Resistance movement in the Rambouillet area. According to Prompsaud, his initial involvement with the Comet Line happened by chance:

I was in my small truck, having just returned from Saint-Léger-en-Yvelines when I saw a man in a military uniform. It was bizarre—he acted like a scared animal: He saw me, and then seemed to hide. I got out of my truck. It was a beautiful day, so I was in a short-sleeved shirt and therefore didn't have my gun on me. Then I noticed the man was in a British uniform. He motioned for me to go into the woods, and then he spoke French.

He was Belgian! He was a member of the Comet Line and from that moment, I became a member of the Comet Line, too.

Prompsaud became known as one of the most charismatic and respected résistants, and was the most powerful member of the Resistance in the area. It was he who recruited my great-grandmother:

I met Madame Le Febvre, whose husband was a prisoner of war. She had two sons who spoke pretty good English, which was a plus. Madame Le Febvre seemed very patriotic, so I decided to pose the question. She was intrigued. I told her, "The biggest mistake you can make is to be observed." She understood immediately. She was an intelligent woman; both she and her sons had common sense.

Whenever the Allies engaged in a mission, members of the Comet Line watched the sky—and so did the Germans. The cell was composed of a vast network of individuals, each with a specialized role, who worked tirelessly to rescue downed airmen before they fell into the hands of the Germans. Prompsaud's carefully chosen setup included a butcher who provided food, a man who lived in a large, secluded house in the woods where Prompsaud hid supplies, and my great-grandmother and two other women who provided accommodations in their homes for the airmen. Prompsaud and a friend personally financed the cost of clothing, shoes, linens, food, tobacco, and sweets for the airmen.

Everyone contributed in their own way to the overall success of the organization. When firemen retrieved fallen airmen, they disguised them using fireman garb; likewise, farmers provided farming attire. Even the mayor of Rambouillet may have indirectly assisted the effort. Prompsaud's report indicates that the mayor supplied a city firetruck for the Resistance and ensured that Christiane's home wasn't requisitioned for use by German occupiers—a situation that would have otherwise been likely given the fact that her home was quite nice and very close to the *Kommandantur* (Commandant's headquarters).

Prompsaud's reports described an intricate, highly organized network. The participants were ordinary people who'd lived normal lives before the war, yet they possessed such indomitable spirit and commitment to the ideals of freedom, they were willing to risk everything they had—including their lives—to defend their liberty. Each document I read echoed these French citizens' determination to fight for their freedom; their bravery and persistence struck a deep chord within me. Their stories dominated my thoughts, and I was fascinated, awed, and proud that my great-grandmother was part of this group.

My discoveries about my great-grandmother Christiane have brought me to this conclusion: Not only was she incredibly courageous, she also was a bit of a rebel. She was a woman with strong personal values who resolved to honor her principles—and fight for freedom—no matter the cost. I believe I have grown up with the same values my ancestors possessed. I was taught that if I'm not happy about something, I should take action rather than placing blame. And that's exactly what Christiane did. I believe she would have done whatever she could to help free her country from the Third Reich's domination. When Monsieur Prompsaud asked my great-grandmother to help, she didn't hesitate to offer her assistance. She did so as a patriot and a mother who could not accept the occupation of France—and the loss of independence—for her country, herself, and her husband, but mostly, for her beloved sons.

My grandmother's sister, Tante (Aunt) Odette, knew Christiane. When I asked her about this daring great-grandmother of mine, she said, "Ma chérie, you know this was a very bad time in the history of our country. Your Great-grandmother, Christiane, was a tough lady with high standards. She took many risks for herself, for her family, and in the name of freedom. And she took those risks even though many people thought her to be an irresponsible mother for doing so."

While some may have thought Christiane to be irresponsible and selfish, I believe Sascha and I would do the same thing in her position. We want our son to have the same luxury throughout his life that we have enjoyed—the luxury of freedom.

While Christiane took huge risks—especially for a mother—Claude was already an adult when Christiane joined the French Underground in the quest for freedom. Yes, he was young, but no younger than many of those who came from the United States—including Russell Cotts and Jack Davis—to fight for freedom on a continent that wasn't their own.

The famous French writer and poet, Antoine de Saint-Exupéry—who, incidentally, traveled to the United States to help persuade the U.S. government to join the fight against the Nazis—wrote, "Ce qui donne un sens à la vie donne un sens à la mort." ("What gives a sense to life, gives a sense to death.") Christiane's courage is a picture of this. She was willing to take great risks because she understood the value of freedom and the meaning it gives to life—and to the potential of death for the sake of recovering that freedom.

Christiane Le Febvre and her son Claude, age 19
Rambouillet, France
August, 1944

CHAPTER THIRTEEN

THREE DAYS WITH MY GREAT-GRANDMOTHER

The risks my great-grandmother was willing to take were worth the cost, not only in the freedom she helped secure, but also in the lives of the airmen she hid and housed. As I read the rest of Amy's account of her father's story, it became evident that he considered her a hero:

> Dad was sheltered in Rambouillet for three days by the Le Febvre family. Mrs. Christiane Le Febvre and her son, Claude, were with the French Underground, and they graciously welcomed him into their home. Mrs. Le Febvre told my father her husband had been captured by the Nazis during the fall of Paris and was imprisoned in Germany.
>
> Dad also discovered he wasn't the only airman the Le Febvres were harboring. "Two other crewmen from my aircraft—the bombardier and the navigator—were already at the house when I arrived," he said. "And another man, an American fighter pilot, had taken refuge with the Le Febvres as well."

During my dad's second day with the family, an additional famil-iar face showed up: the bombing mission's ball turret gunner. The men alternated their time between the indoors and the Le Feb-vre's back yard, which was enclosed by a large stone wall. As they waited for their next move, the U.S. Eighth Air Force[15] bombed Rambouillet's railroad station, and the men could see the air-planes and hear the bombing. It was terrifying for them to hear the sound of fighter planes diving on the target and feel the boom of the explosions.

On his third morning at the Le Febvre home, members of the French Underground appeared and told Dad he was leaving. He thanked Mrs. Le Febvre and Claude, said good-bye, and left with his new escort. As I mentioned earlier, Dad didn't speak French and was warned not to talk as he and his guide began a se-ries of moves back to Paris. I was a bit surprised when my dad, whom I considered to be big and strong, admitted he felt scared and vulnerable. "I had no control over the situation, and I was dependent on others. German troops were all over the place, particularly in Rambouillet and Paris, and I kept thinking they'd see right through my deception. After all, I knew I was an Ameri-can, and I felt sure the Germans could recognize that, too," he said. These thoughts haunted Dad as he and his French protec-tor took an inter-urban train into the city and stayed there for the night. Dad recalled catching sight of the Eiffel Tower as it loomed on the horizon. He said it was a mesmerizing vision, but of course, he didn't have time—or the desire— to linger. He just wanted to reach safety.

The next day, my dad and his French companion boarded an-other train. To discourage conversation from other travelers, he pretended to read a newspaper. At one stop, a passenger stood up, grabbed his parcel from the overhead luggage rack, and dropped it right on top of my dad. He apologized profusely as Dad sat anxiously and said nothing. The train meandered

---

15   Historical records indicate that the Ninth Air Force bombed the Rambouillet train station.

through the countryside, and my dad and his escort finally got off. They spent the night at a nearby farm, and Dad hid in the hayloft of the barn. It's a good thing he was tucked away. During the night, German soldiers retreating from the Allies stopped at the farmhouse in search of bicycles. They didn't believe the farmer's family when they told them there were none, and the Nazis combed the lower level of the barn several times. All my dad could do was hold his breath and pray the soldiers wouldn't climb into the loft. Needless to say, he didn't get much sleep that night.

Dad had another close call the next day as they walked through a wheat field toward the American lines. When he and his guide came to a fork in the road, they headed right. "We'd gone a few hundred yards past the intersection when a German armored vehicle approached and took the left fork. It suddenly screeched to a halt, backed up, and barreled right toward us. I remember thinking that we were doomed. Surely this time our luck had run out, and the Germans knew I was an escapee! But the Germans drove right past us and, once again, we evaded capture," he said.

As they drew closer to the front, my dad's French escort bade him farewell and told him the U.S. army wasn't too far down the road. Dad continued alone for a few miles before spying a welcome sight—an American ambulance. He jumped into the middle of the road frantically waving his arms, and the driver almost ran him down. My dad raced to the side of the vehicle, pulled out his dog tags, and told the driver he was an American B-17 pilot who'd been shot down and was escaping capture. The driver motioned Dad into the front seat, and as they sped away the driver told him he was carrying several badly wounded French Resistance fighters to the hospital. One later died. After a short ride, the ambulance left my dad with a group attached to the U.S. Fifth Division. He knew he was very lucky to be back with American forces. He was sent to England, where he met Ed O'Day, the bombardier. Having escaped capture with the help of the French Resistance, neither O'Day nor my dad would serve again in Europe. Both men were sent back to the United States. My dad became an instructor pilot for the B-17, and also joined the U.S. Air Transport Command and ferried fighter planes from aircraft plants to military air bases throughout the United States.

Dad was eventually told that the pilot was captured by the Germans and reported as a prisoner of war, and the four men who'd bailed out with him had died. As for the navigator and bombardier who had been at the Le Febvre home with him, Dad didn't know what happened to them.

My Dad wasn't alone: Although over half of the airmen on that B-17 bomber had made it home, it seems that none of them knew the fate of the others. I have a feeling that many of them assumed that the others had perished. Perhaps they didn't want to know. They had all experienced loss and many of them may have wanted to put the war behind them, whether they went home or continued serving in the military. And, it was much harder to track people down then than it is now. However, in the 1980s, thanks to an article in Airmen Magazine, my dad learned that Ed O-Day was looking for him. The two men finally got in touch four decades after their plane had crashed over France.

Although he was the last person off the B-17 and made sure the rest of the crew had exited the plane before he jumped, my dad never considered himself a hero. To him, the real heroes were twofold: the men who didn't return from a mission and would never be going home, and the men and women of the French Resistance, to whom he was eternally grateful. As my dad emphasized countless times, these people were willing to sacrifice all to assist Allied troops whom they didn't know. They knew their very lives could be ended in an instant should their Resistance activity be revealed—which could easily happen by a mere slip of the tongue—yet they bravely continued to put their lives on the line.

He called them the most courageous people he'd ever met.

I was still absorbing the idea that I was related to these incredibly courageous people, but another feeling was replacing my surprise: pride. The more I learned about my great-grandmother and grandfather, the more proud I felt, and the more I was driven to discover their story.

Le Febvre Family Garden
Standing (from left): Claude Le Febvre, John Larkin
Seated (from left): James Lindquist, Jack Davis, Christiane Le Febvre,
Russell Cotts, Edward O'Day
Rambouillet, France
August, 1944

CHAPTER FOURTEEN

MORE DISCOVERIES

Through my research into the Comet Line I made an important discovery. As I perused wartime documentation registered under Grand-père Claude's name, I discovered Christiane had hidden two more pilots in her home from June 13 until July 9, 1944. Kenneth Walter Chapman, a British citizen, and New Zealander Philip John Lamason stayed for almost a month before they were moved to another house. Sadly, the two men were captured by the Germans as they were being taken out of the occupied zone. Both were sent to Buchenwald where, according to prisoners, the only way to escape the camp was through the "smoke of the chimney." From what I've learned about life—and death—in concentration camps, those words gave me the chills.

The good news is both men survived the war and were able to return home. One passed away in 2008 and the other in 2012. I'm sorry I didn't have the opportunity to speak with them, but Lamason's file contained an extraordinary piece of information—a link to "lostairmen.com." I clicked on the site link and watched an amazing teaser for "Lost Airmen of Buchenwald," a documentary made by Mike Dorsey, the grandson of one of the 168 captured pilots who were interned there. I think I may have literally jumped up and down with joy. At any rate, I was on cloud nine and immediately ordered the DVD.

It seems that every time I hit a brick wall in my research, another avenue opens; and, that's exactly what this wonderful documentary turned out to be. I ordered the film from my home in Berlin and waited impatiently for it to arrive. A week later, when the postman delivered my package, I dropped everything I was doing and slipped the DVD into the player.

It's difficult to imagine such betrayal, but the documentary describes how 168 Allied pilots were "sold out" by one fake résistant. As I watched, the face of an old man, identified as Lamason, appeared on the screen, and for me, time stood still. There, in my living room, was a pilot who'd stayed at Christiane's home—a solid link to the past. I felt as if he spoke directly to me as he and others described the emotions they felt and what they'd experienced as their planes fell from the sky. I paid close attention to their tales of escape, and then capture; their time at Buchenwald; how they organized themselves in order to survive. One of the most interesting things these men talked about was how German pilots came to their defense so the Allied pilots wouldn't be treated as spies, but rather, as prisoners of war. As mere prisoners, they'd be treated less harshly and have a greater chance of survival. It's ironic, but in a way, these pilots owed their lives to their enemies—which goes to show the strong bonds of kinship that unite the flying community.

These "Lost Airmen" survived nightmarish conditions, and their story was kept secret for over sixty years. Although Lamason passed away a few months after he was interviewed, this enthralling tribute to an unforgettable group of men inspired me to seek more information. Right after I viewed the film, I sent an email to Mike Dorsey thanking him for the remarkable work he'd produced. I felt close to him because he was the grandson of one of those airmen. I also asked him if he had any unused footage of Lamason's interview. Less than forty-eight hours later, I received a reply and a link to Lamason's entire conversation.

Although I'd hoped to learn more about his stay at Christiane's, the uncut footage of Lamason's interview revealed nothing more about the subject. But I gained so much from watching it. This gentle man exhibited dignity, humility, and a wonderful sense of humor even as he described the horror he had endured. I felt as if I truly knew this man, and I also understood exactly how lucky he was to have survived the war.

The story of Russell Cotts' escape to the free zone made more sense to me now. He faced petrifying danger and had to rely on strangers. How difficult it must have been for him to be stranded in an unfamiliar land, to place his life in the hands of someone he didn't know, to be unable to communicate with others because he didn't speak the language, to be surrounded by enemies!

CHAPTER FIFTEEN

TO CHRISTIANE'S AND HOME AGAIN

A second lightbulb clicked on for me when I read about the August 2, 1944 flight of the 385th Bomb Group on the Comet Line website:

> *Five men manage to escape: Russell J. Cotts ... the bombardier Edward O'Day ... the radio operator T / Sgt Marion T. Church ... the navigator 2nd Lt. James I. Lindquist ... and the ventral ball turret gunner S / Sgt Jack C. Davis ... .*

> *The fall of the plane [was] observed [not only] by German troops, but also by members of the resistance.*[16]

The website went on mention my great-grandmother by name and list the dates that she'd hosted several airmen in her home, but my mind was still on that first sentence. *Russell Cotts and Jack Davis had been on the same plane!* Not only had the two airmen both found

---

16 Comète Kinship Belgium. *Aviateurs alliés rassemblés en camps de Comète.* Retrieved from http://www.cometeline.org/ficheD372.html

shelter in my great-grandmother's home, it was there that they were reunited after their plane had disintegrated in the air.

The second half of Jack Davis' story reveals a bit more about how these two men's stories intertwined:

Mrs. Le Febvre's home was a beautiful two-story with a basement. She greeted me when I arrived and had me sign a log book. I later met Mrs. Le Febvre's son, Claude—who came and went during my stay—but, regretfully, I never met her husband. He was a colonel in the French army, and had been captured by the Germans early in the war. Mrs. Le Febvre escorted me into the living room of her home where I met four other American airmen: a P-51 pilot and three officers from my own crew—the navigator, James Lindquist, the bombardier, Edward O'Day, and our co-pilot, Russell Cotts.

Not much happened after my arrival there, though the one thing that stands out in my memory is that we ate potato soup nearly every day. Mrs. Le Febvre owned a German shepherd that was trained to dig potatoes, and we spent many hours in the backyard with the dog digging for our food. The other men and I had been at the Le Febvre home for about three days when we were informed that guides would escort three of us out of France. We drew straws to determine who'd get to go and, naturally, I lost. Cotts, Lindquist, and O'Day pulled the longest straws. During that evening, the P-51 pilot (who'd also lost the draw) and I watched German soldiers pull artillery toward the Rambouillet forest and listened as the sounds of gunfire echoed throughout the night. The next morning, Mrs. Le Febvre rushed into our room and told us the Americans had arrived and the Germans had fled. We were all overjoyed, of course, and now that the danger had passed, Mrs. Le Febvre was eager to take the two of us to town and show us off.

We arrived in town after a short walk and were greeted by residents. One shop owner smashed the front window of his business, which had been padlocked, and climbed through the broken shards of glass. After a few minutes, he came out and presented me with a bottle of French perfume to take home to my wife. Just as I thanked him, a person hurried over to Mrs. Le Febvre and began speaking excitedly. She immediately hustled us back to her house and told us the Germans were supposedly launching a counter attack at Chartres[17] and Rambouillet was in the direct path of the attack. We later discovered this was merely a rumor, not true at all, and we thanked God.

That night the town held a celebration the organizers called the Liberation of Rambouillet Banquet. Since the P-51 pilot and I were the only remaining Allied forces in Rambouillet, we were the guests of honor. It didn't seem to matter that we'd had nothing to do with the Liberation, and we were just happy to feast on lunch meat, fruit, wine, and homemade bread after a steady diet of potato soup.

We walked back to town the next morning and met several of Mrs. Le Febvre's friends. As we headed back to her house, a Jeep pulled alongside us, and one of the passengers asked for directions to the Le Febvre residence. We introduced ourselves, and the men told us they'd come to transport two American airmen. I remember wondering at the time how they knew we were at the Le Febvre home, and I was later told Claude Le Febvre had slipped through enemy lines prior to the liberation of Rambouillet and notified American officers of our presence. We returned to Mrs. Le Febvre's house, uttered tearful good-byes, climbed into the Jeep, and began the slow process of returning home.

The occupants of the jeep were special forces personnel who'd come to France two weeks prior to D-Day. Their mission was to blow up bridges and ammunition supply trucks, and attack other targets. The men drove the pilot and me to a POW collection

---

17   Chartres is forty-five kilometers from Rambouillet.

point about thirty miles south of Rambouillet and turned us over to American troops. At first, we were treated as POWs, which was a bit unsettling. We slept just outside the barbed wire enclosures that housed German POWs, and were told to stay put at night. The guards had orders to fire at anything that moved, and if we didn't want to get shot, we needed to alert them when we had to relieve ourselves.

After two days of interrogations and long Jeep and truck rides, we finally arrived in Cherbourg, where we were no longer treated as POWs. An Air Force colonel told us he was going to be leaving for England in a few hours and invited us to go with him if we wanted. Best news ever.

We arrived in England, and I was once again questioned by an intelligence officer. This time I was asked to supply the names of all the French citizens who'd helped me. The officer also questioned me about the amount of food I'd eaten, the clothing I'd been given, and any other help I'd received. I understand the U.S. reimbursed French individuals who'd sheltered and assisted servicemen until they returned to safety. In my opinion, they certainly deserved the compensation. The next thing I did was send a telegram to Jerry, telling her that I was all right and would see her very soon. I was given an escape and evasion number. Then I was sent back to Great Ashfield, where my thirty-second mission had begun, to pick up the personal effects I'd left there. I secured my final pay, and reported to an airfield in London for a flight home.

I landed at Bolling Field in Washington, D.C., and was interrogated once again—this time by a colonel stationed at the Pentagon. When the questioning was finished, a finance officer arranged for my transportation home. With ticket in hand, I finally boarded a train to my final destination—Little Rock, Arkansas. The trip seemed to take forever, but I'll never forget my feelings of joy when I saw Jerry and Janie waiting for me at the station. Home at last.

Forty years have passed since that fateful thirty-second mission, and some memories and details are now hazier than others. But one thing I am sure of is that I never lost faith: I knew I would return home and be reunited with the two people whom I loved more than anything. Looking back, I know the ending of this story could have been very different. What if one of the German officers on the subway had spoken to me? Would I have panicked? What if one of the houses I had stayed in had been checked? There I was in someone else's clothes with no identification. I probably would have been shot right along with the French Underground member. Believe me, I've thanked the Lord many times that this didn't happen.

As I write this account, I hope my children and grandchildren will heed my words. Always keep faith—and when things look the darkest, always remember there's light at the end of the tunnel.

And finally, never, ever forget: Although hundreds of airmen were returned home by brave members of the Underground, thousands were shot down and never lived to make that sweet journey home. I'll remember them the rest of my life.

Jack Davis never forgot those who sacrificed all for the sake of freedom, and many remembered him for his unwavering service and generosity. Jimmy Davis, Jack Davis' son, describes his father as a well-loved man of integrity:

Although Daddy was only five feet, four inches tall, he was a gentle giant among the masses, and a valiant warrior in combat. He never wavered in his duties to God, family, country, and friends. I remember my grandmother (Daddy's Mother) telling me of a time during the depression when they had little more to eat than what they grew in a small garden. Yet, Daddy asked for food to give to one of his "poor" friends at school. He took a jar of home-canned green beans to his friend the next day. This was Daddy: He always gave with a happy heart.

He fought in the skies during WWII and on land in Korea; and, he was a soldier in the trenches of Nevada during Operation Tumbler-Snapper in 1952, participating in the testing of eight atomic bomb blasts. Daddy was commissioned as an officer after WWII, and rose in rank through Korea and the U.S. Army Reserves until his retirement as a Colonel. He never wavered or complained. All who knew him loved him.

Several years after his death, one of the officers Daddy served with in Korea called to tell my mother how much he thought of Daddy as a man and a soldier. He said, "Jack Davis was a man's man, and the greatest warrior I have ever known." Daddy taught me that doing what is right may not be the easiest path to take, but it is the only path to take.

CHAPTER SIXTEEN

LIBERATION

Maman received Amy Cotts' letter in 2010, and three years passed before I fully committed to piecing together Christiane and Claude's story. I'll never know all the specifics—for example, how they reacted to particular events, what inspired them to take certain actions—but my journey of discovery is an ongoing one that continues even as I write these words.

I yearned to know more about the liberation of Rambouillet and in doing some online research in January 2015, I landed on the French website for the *Musée de la Résistance* (Museum of the Resistance). When I entered "Rambouillet" into the search bar of the site, I was delightfully surprised to discover that an entire book had been written on the topic. *The Liberation of Rambouillet,* France was authored by Françoise Winieska, an American citizen born in France who happens to be one of Europe's most respected photographers of French gardens and wildflowers.[18]   I went directly to Amazon. I was surprised

---

18   Taylor, Lois. (1997, July 18). Gardens of France. *Honolulu Star-Bulletin.* Retrieved from http://archives.starbulletin.com/97/07/22/features/evergreen.html

and a bit disappointed to learn that very few copies of Madame Winieska's book were available, and not a single one was available in France. There was one available in the United States, but it cost $70.00. I ordered a copy from a seller in Australia and patiently waited for more than two weeks for this precious book to arrive.

After reading the book, I was determined to get in touch with Madame Winieska to see if she could provide me with any additional information. (She was born in 1933, and I was crossing my fingers that she was still alive.) I searched the Internet and also contacted SHARY, the association that published the book, but I didn't hear back from them. Unfortunately for me, I'd tried to get in touch with them in May, a month which contains several French national holidays, and the SHARY offices were closed. My next course of action was to contact Monsieur Gérard Larcher, the man who wrote the book's introduction in 1999. At that time, he was the mayor of Rambouillet; today, he's the president of the French Senate. His assistant found an old U.S. address for Madame Winieska, but it seemed she no longer lived there. I'd exhausted almost every avenue and wasn't sure where I'd turn next when, once again, luck intervened: A representative of SHARY finally responded to my inquiry and offered to put me in touch with Madame Winieska. Shortly after our conversation, I was thrilled to receive a phone call from the author herself!

Madame Winieska insisted we address each other on a first-name basis and told me that she lived both in Rambouillet and in the United States. She was currently in France (another stroke of luck!), so we agreed to meet in Rambouillet when I travelled to Paris for business a few weeks later. I'm honored to say we became friends from the start, and I found her to be an absolute delight: full of passion and joy. I'm very grateful to Françoise for so generously giving me permission to use her book as the primary reference for this chapter.

As I read this well-researched and detailed account of the four days of the liberation of Rambouillet, I tried to picture what my family members had experienced: *Where were they when certain events occurred? What were they thinking? Were they afraid?* I was able to uncover some of the answers, thanks to my many hours of research and the generous help of others; but for the unanswered questions, I've had to use my imagination.

In the second week of August 1944, General Patton's Third United States Army began liberating French towns as it made its way toward the Seine River. Epernon, a town less than fourteen kilometers from Rambouillet, was being liberated, the Americans were approaching Rambouillet, and the Germans wanted to push them back. Additional German troops arrived in Rambouillet on August 15, joining the others already entrenched in the town. The Germans had commandeered a farm owned by Monsieur Baron and were using the property as headquarters for their infantry regiment. The Kommandantur was ensconced at 11 rue Gambetta. Christiane was only four-tenths of a mile from the Kommandantur and about the same distance from the Baron Farm—just a few minutes' walk to either place. Although she was living in a precarious location, I like to think she had a bit of protection since her home was somewhat off the beaten path.

This map of Rambouillet shows the Baron Farm, the Kommandantur, the Château de Rambouillet, and Great-grandmother Christiane's home.

Map of Rambouillet showing the short distances between the home of Christiane LeFebvre, the Kommandantur, the Baron Farm, and the Château de Rambouillet.

On the afternoon of August 16, the Germans took four citizens of Rambouillet hostage—including a Monsieur Picard and his fifteen-year-old son—and held them at the Baron Farm. Approximately thirty minutes later, an American reconnaissance unit of ten men in three vehicles entered at the western entrance of town, (on the road to Gazeran, Épernon, Maintenon, and Chartres). However, this unit was ambushed at a roadblock set up by the Germans, killing three soldiers and leaving three wounded, including a sergeant. As the American vehicles sped through Rambouillet, many of its citizens thought the town was being liberated, but they soon discovered otherwise. I can't help but wonder what Christiane must have been thinking when she heard the gunfire. Jack Davis and James Lindquist were still with her. And where was Grand-père? With the help of a résistant, the Americans in their armored vehicle shot their way out of Rambouillet.

The next day the Germans took another hostage, a priest; and, at 5:30 in the afternoon, they brought a fifth hostage to the Kommandantur in exchange for the release of the young man. The Kommandant told the priest that the Germans planned to leave Rambouillet, and the hostages would be used as shields: If any German soldiers were killed during their exit from the town, the hostages would be shot. *I wonder if Christiane knew that her fellow citizens, including a priest, had been taken hostage.*

American forces arrived at the village of Gazeran (which by then was free of German forces), two and a half kilometers west of Rambouillet, on the morning of August 18. Those same forces, consisting of forty vehicles transporting approximately one hundred fifty soldiers, were divided into two groups that were to attack Rambouillet: one from the west and the other from the north. Expecting the American forces, the Germans established roadblocks at the western entrance to the town, and greeted the forces with artillery fire. The fighting was fierce, and both sides suffered casualties. When I learned this, I was reminded of a comment in Jack Davis' briefing, "During the night the German soldiers were pulling artillery toward the Rambouillet forest, and we heard artillery fire most of the night." The tension must have been agonizing.

Back at the Kommandantur, the hostages witnessed increased activity in the courtyard as the Germans made preparations to depart.

Finally, just after 9:00 p.m., the Kommandant addressed the captives. "We are leaving," he said. "I am reminding you that you are my men's warranty. You will be pitilessly shot to the last one if a single shot is fired, but I trust the population. I am going to entrust you to the officer commanding the regiment. He will free you once the last soldier is gone."[19] With that, Germans wielding rifles and submachine guns surrounded the hostages and escorted them into the silent, deserted street. They were shepherded to Monsieur Baron's farm, where the Kommandant shook hands with each of them and left. Several trucks carrying German soldiers and equipment followed. At 10:45 p.m., the German officer commanding the regiment freed the hostages, and then left Rambouillet.

When the sun rose over Rambouillet on Saturday, August 19, 1944, the town was free of Germans for the first time in more than four years. But the liberation was not without casualties: Nine Americans had been killed in the town during the previous three days.

The first American to arrive in Rambouillet after the liberation was the world-renown writer Ernest Hemingway, who was a war correspondent for *Collier's Magazine.* He described his initial observations in "Battle for Paris," an article published in the September 30, 1944 issue. "At the outpost of the regiment we found some Frenchmen who had just come in from Rambouillet by bicycle [...] they informed me that the last Germans had left at three o'clock that morning but that the roads into the town were mined." He continued, "When I reached the outpost again, I found two cars full of French guerrilla fighters, most of whom were naked to the waist. They were armed with pistols and two Sten guns they had received by parachute. They had just come from Rambouillet and their story of the German withdrawal tallied with the information other French had given." *Was Grand-père one of these "French guerillas" to whom Hemingway referred, or the one who informed him that the Germans had just left? This prospect intrigued me. By the afternoon of the nineteenth, Rambouillet was*

---

19   Winieska, Françoise. (1999). *August 1944: The Liberation of Rambouillet, France.* Rambouillet, France: SHARY.

bursting with members of the American military, the Secret Service, special services, and the press; and most, including Hemingway, had settled into the Hôtel du Grand Veneur.

The influx of people continued the next day. According to an article in the Paris newspaper, *Le Parisien,* more Americans arrived in Rambouillet on the morning of August 20, and that evening there was a gala in front of city hall.[20] *That must have been the celebration Jack Davis attended with Christiane and the pilot!* Although Davis never mentioned that Grand-père attended the celebration, he did say Grand-père was the one who alerted American officers that he and the pilot were hidden at Christiane's home. *When and how did Grand-père share this information with the Americans?*

Thanks to the American reconnaissance mission, the Germans had suddenly departed from Christiane and Grand-père's town, and August 19, 1944, was a joyful day in Rambouillet—but not in Paris. When Parisians heard news of the Allies' quick advance, they were confident their city would soon be liberated. Citizens brazenly rose up against the Germans, an act that resulted in the deaths of 1,500 Parisians.[21] And although those brave souls sacrificed their lives for freedom, the City of Light was still under German control. The liberation of Paris would take a coordinated effort by French and American forces—and Grand-père and his fellow résistants would play an instrumental role.

The Liberation of Paris

Rambouillet became a hotbed of activity during the days following the town's liberation. American troops marched through the streets and were cheered by jubilant citizens. Journalists and photographers from publications such as *Life Magazine, Newsweek,* and The Saturday Evening Post poured into town accompanied by reporters from the As-

---

20   *Le Parisien.* (2014, August 19). *La Difficile Entrée des Américains dans Rambouillet.* Retrieved from http://www.leparisien.fr/espace-premium/yvelines-78/
21   Trueman, Chris. *The Liberation of Paris.* Retrieved from http://www.historylearningsite. co.uk/

sociated Press and other news organizations. They crowded into the Hôtel du Grand Veneur along with high-ranking military personnel.

By this time, Operation Overlord was almost over. The objective of this Allied military campaign was to trap the Germans between three rivers and decimate their forces before they could cross the Seine. The Allies planned to bypass Paris for tactical reasons, but de Gaulle was determined to change the Allies' course of action, as the liberation of Paris was crucial to his own political ambitions. He returned to France on August 20 from England and met with Eisenhower in an unsuccessful attempt to convince the general of the importance of liberating Paris. De Gaulle did not take this rejection lightly. The next evening, he sent a letter to Eisenhower threatening to take matters into his own hands. De Gaulle wrote that he planned to use the French Second Armored Division, led by General Leclerc, to accomplish his mission. (Leclerc and his troops had landed at Utah Beach in Normandy three weeks earlier, on August 1, 1944, to join General Patton's Third U.S. Army.) After receiving de Gaulle's ultimatum, Eisenhower and American deputy commander General Bradley engaged in nonstop meetings for the next one and a half days and brought in a member of the Paris Resistance general staff to share his perspective on the situation in Paris. He told the generals the French capital had been in an open state of revolt for more than five days. General von Choltitz, the German commander in charge of Paris, had agreed to a truce until August 23, but Resistance leaders feared the worst would happen when the truce ended. In fact, Hitler had ordered von Choltitz to blow up and destroy the entire city of Paris. He said, "Paris muss brennen." ("Paris must burn.") Von Choltitz had prepared to follow orders by installing explosives. However, the general was reluctant to carry out this directive thanks to Swedish diplomat Raoul Nordling, who had persuaded him to spare the City of Light. Had Hitler gotten wind of von Choltitz's plan to save the city, he would have immediately replaced the general with someone more "cooperative." Over a decade later, in 1955, von Choltitz received the *Medal Chevallier d'Honneur* from the French Government to thank him for protecting Paris from destruction.

On the evening of August 22, General Bradley gave the order to Leclerc to march on Paris. Leclerc and his Second Armored Division were to attack Paris from the west, and the American 4th Infantry Division—led by General Gerow—from the south. General Leclerc and some of his staff arrived in Rambouillet on August 23. Ironically, they established their headquarters at the former Kommandantur, which had housed five hostages only one week earlier. Meanwhile, preparations were underway for de Gaulle's arrival that evening at the Château de Rambouillet. His car stopped in front of City Hall, and he stepped out to cheers from a crowd of residents. Town officials, including Monsieur Prompsaud, greeted him, and he gave speeches to the ecstatic crowd. In my heart, I'm certain Christiane was among those in the crowd. De Gaulle walked to the château, and shortly thereafter, he met with Leclerc. The two men discussed the impending march on Paris, and Leclerc informed De Gaulle that he intended to ignore part of Gerow's original orders and had modified the route his troops would take. De Gaulle supported the revised plan, and the two French generals then finalized a political strategy for the country once Paris was free.

General Leclerc, his Second Armored Division, and Resistance members left Rambouillet at dawn on August 24. Paris was liberated on August 25, 1944 by the French, the Americans, and   other Allied nations. De Gaulle departed Rambouillet by car at 2:00 p.m. that very day and entered a liberated—and jubilant—Paris.

Grand-père's Role

Grand-père was among those determined Resistance fighters who helped liberate the capital. He marched with General Leclerc from Rambouillet into the streets of Paris and fought alongside his fellow patriots. Two days before the Liberation, members of the Resistance (which, by this time, was called the FFI: French Forces of the Interior), started freeing all French civilians who were held as prisoners in the capital city—and the Germans counterattacked. The fighting continued as French and American forces, including my grandfather, entered the city. His heroism as a Resistance fighter was documented in a July 14, 1946 article published in La Tribune Républicaine, a newspaper from the Rambouillet region.

We were happy to learn of the distinction that has just been bestowed upon our friend Claude Le Febvre: The Croix de Guerre with two silver stars was the well-deserved reward for Le Febvre's actions during the Occupation and the Liberation.

As a member of the FFI, Le Febvre made diverse missions from June 9 through August 19, 1944, during which time he was arrested twice. He marched on Paris with the troops of General Leclerc, entering the capital city during the night of August 24. On August 25, while clearing a building occupied by the enemy, he was hit by machine gun fire, though he nevertheless continued to fight.

Claude Le Febvre, who celebrated his twenty-first birthday only three days ago, was decorated during the July 14 festivities; the joyous day ended with his engagement to Miss Jeannine Villet, daughter of Attorney and Mrs. André Villet of Rambouillet.

The Tribune Républicaine offers its congratulations and wishes much happiness to Jeannine Villet and Claude Le Febvre.

My heart seemed to swell in my chest as when I first read these words. My grandfather had helped liberate Paris—*my Grand-père!* I was hit with a new wave of pride in my family and a new determination to learn more about my family's heritage of courage.

Honoring Fallen Americans

On Sunday, August 26, 1944, the first official ceremony to honor the American soldiers killed at the entrance of Rambouillet was held at the site of the ambush, near the graves where the men were buried. The young men's families had yet to be notified of their deaths by American authorities, and the town's inhabitants acted as surrogates for the relatives and friends of these brave soldiers who'd traveled so far and died on foreign soil. Together, the community gathered and paid homage to these heroes who'd lost their lives on Rambouillet's doorstep fighting for their freedom.

In 1944, a commemorative pillar was erected at the site of the August 16 ambush. A permanent memorial (*Le Monument du Souvenir et de la Reconnaissance*) was unveiled on June 1, 1947, and soon became known by the citizens of Rambouillet as *Le Monument Américain*. It reads:

In Memory of the American Soldiers
Who Fell for the Liberation
of Our Region in August 1944

Every year, on August 19, Rambouillet holds a ceremony at the monument. I will attend the ceremony for the first time with Françoise Winieska.

Claude Le Febvre (in white t-shirt) during the Liberation of
Paris. August 24, 1944. Paris, France

CHAPTER SEVENTEEN

DEAR RUSSELL

The number of documents I received from Amy on American Mother's Day, May 12, 2013, was mind-boggling—as was the information they contained. As Amy's emails continued to stream into my inbox, I discovered copies of letters written by both Christiane and Claude to Russell Cotts. As I read the letters, I was flabbergasted: My family had corresponded with Amy's dad for more than fifty years!

How strange it felt to discover so much information about my own family from a total stranger who lived an ocean away. I was discovering my family's private thoughts and dreams, like my grandfather's feelings for my grandmother (then his girlfriend) and his hope to become a pilot. My family had never mentioned any of these things, but someone I'd never met had given me a wealth of connections to my past. I even found a letter in which my dad talked about my siblings and me as teenagers.

I was extremely grateful for every detail I learned, of course, but I doubt anyone could ever be prepared for this experience. It took me a few days to absorb all the information, and then I received another email from Amy. She told me she'd found more documents. Attached was a photo of my grandparents and their two sons, which was taken on the beach in Normandy. My dad appeared to be two or three years old at the time. I was touched—it was so personal. The fact that my grandfather had sent such an intimate family picture to Amy's father confirmed the very unique and special relationship that linked the two men.

Amy also sent a copy of a New Year's card my dad had written. I hadn't read anything in his handwriting since he'd passed away, and seeing my dad's familiar script filled me with both sorrow and joy. I cried for what must have been the hundredth time, but I also smiled as happy memories replaced the sadness. Inside, my dad had written a note to the Cotts asking if they knew of a family my brother could stay with for a while in order to improve his English. I laughed out loud: My brother's English was never very good when he was young, and it's not much better today. That's why Maman gave *me* Amy's letter in the first place.

Amy tells me her dad initiated their correspondence by obtaining Christiane's address from the U.S. Army. Grand-père Claude responded in either French or English, but all of Christiane's replies were in French—so Amy says her father took the letters to the local university for translation. Christiane always addressed him as "Mon petit John." John was Russell Cotts' middle name, and "mon petit" is one of countless French terms of endearment; it literally means "my little," though a comparable English phrase would be "my sweet."

I was excited to read the letters Christiane and Claude had written to their friend—an American who had spent only three days in their home. Through their words, I feel I've come to better understand who my great-grandmother and grandfather were, and the ideals they held dear. I'm delighted to share parts of their letters with you.

Rambouillet, 18 July 1945

Mon petit John,

Please excuse me for writing in French, but I speak your language badly and you wouldn't understand me. How nice of you not to have forgotten us. Thank your mother and father for their kind words, and tell them there is no need to thank us. I did what was natural and in my place, they would have done the same.

I was lucky until the end, and on the 19ᵗʰ of August when Rambouillet was liberated, I still had Jack Davis and James [in my house].

Jack has written to me and his letter, like yours, has brought me more joy than you can imagine—great, great joy. But James doesn't remember us any longer, nor does Edward, though I loved them, too, like my own children.

You were under my protection, and like a mother hen I never wanted anything bad to happen to my little chicks; I couldn't have lived with myself!

Claude is waiting to get into the Air Force any day now. I'm a bit sad to see him go, since he was my companion during these unfortunate days and, without his presence, my days would have been really terrible. But that's life. He is engaged to Jeannine. Did you know that?

My other son is still in Paris where he works. My husband came back, seriously slimmed down because they used to eat potato skins. For an entire year, the Germans didn't give them their parcels. Fourteen packages that I sent weren't given to him. (Why do you feed the Germans so well? They did not respect the Geneva Convention.) Unfortunately, we know them well. And we know that you are very good to them. Had they been the victors, you would find out how they would thank you.

Maybe we will occupy them. And I assure you that I would be sure to repossess what they've taken from us: clothes, linens, valuables … And the same thing goes for food—my children and my husband were starving. I was, too, but I never admitted it.

My dear John, they have done so much we can never forget!

And torture ... those who were captured are now coming back, and they are talking. What HORROR! For men to do such things, may they all be cursed! And this comes from me, a Catholic.

My little John, when I had you and your comrades staying with me, you were sheltered in my home and in my heart. When I saw Germans passing in the street right under my window, you cannot imagine the things I used to say to them in my thoughts ... "If only you knew what I have here! If you could take them, together with us, what would you do? Torture them? Shoot them? But you will never have them. I know that I will save them! You vultures of human flesh, you will not take my children. They have been given to me by heaven, and I will return them to their parents."

In my heart, I can feel only hatred for all they have done to us, and what they continue to do.

I'm sending you a few pictures, and I think you'll like them.

We're having fabulous weather, but the farmers say it's too warm and the wheat is getting dry. All of the vegetables are withering, but I wouldn't dare say that the sun is too hot since we are going to freeze again during winter without coal, clothes, and shoes.

I've written such a long letter, I think it will take you two hours to read it! I'm trying to hurry and my writing is poor.

Come see us John, with your parents, and let me hold you tight, John, my boy. My house is yours, and there is still some good wine. The Germans did not find all our hiding places.

Please give my warmest wishes to your parents and thank them for their kind letter.

Ch. Le Febvre

18 July 1945

My dear Russell,

I apologize for taking so long to answer to your letter, but many wonderful events have come during the last two months. My father has come back home from Germany in a [B-17] Flying Fortress, and I am enlisted in the French Air Force. I turned twenty years old on July 13, and then on the 14ᵗʰ, we had the celebration of our National Day. I have been very busy.

It was a wonderful surprise to open your letter and see your picture. You are splendid—just wonderful in your airman's uniform. I hope to go to the U.S.A to do my stage of airman.

Well, my dear fellow, it is late in the evening, and I am tired. I shall write you longer next week, but I see I have forgotten to tell you about the greatest event of my life: I am engaged with Jeannine, my blond girl that you have met in my home! I'm happy to be so lucky!

Now my dear Russell, I shake your hand and stay your French friend for always,

Claude le Febvre

Though Paris was liberated on August 25, 1944, the war continued until Germany's surrender on May 7, 1945—and the nation that had occupied France and other countries during the war was then occupied by the four major Allies.

From Christiane and Claude's letters, I learned that almost two months passed before Grand-père à Chapeau returned home from Germany, but he didn't stay there for long. A short time later, he went back to the country that had once detained him as a prisoner of war—this time as an occupier with his wife by his side.

Rambouillet, 18 September 1945

Mon petit John,

I want to give you my future address because I will be joining my husband in Germany. He is already there, and I'm very happy to be joining him as we will be in a beautiful part of the country.

Would you come to see us? What are you doing now? Are you still in the Air Force?

I always have a picture of you in the back of my mind—it's when you were sitting on the bench in the garden. It's the most beautiful memory, and my heart often thanks you all, the children who came to free us. I believed during those very sad years that I might never see France as a free country again, or my husband alive.

Give your parents my regards, and for you, my dearest John, all my affection.

Ch. Le Febvre

Germany, 11 January 1946

Mon petit John,

You cannot imagine how much your memories and warm wishes, and those of your parents, have moved me. Certainly, when you stayed at my home, I considered you like my son, for did you not all come to save us? So, wasn't it the most natural thing that I would do the same for you? Had the reverse happened, your parents would have done the same. But, what warms my heart is that you have not forgotten us and for that, I send you a big thank you from France.

Yes, my husband has slimmed down a lot, but freedom has brought back some of his cheerfulness, and he has gained some weight. We have been in Germany since October, as part of the occupation. Right now we're on leave, but will return to Germany shortly. My life is very different there: I don't have a lot to do, and I almost forget those terrible days when the Germans were in France. It's funny how the passage of time changes things. After crying of hunger, sadness, discouragement, and fatigue, life turns around. But the future is still dark: We have bad neighbors and life is too expensive in France.

Claude went into the Air Force last year. He has been nominated for the "Croix de Guerre." (I told you he was fired upon in Paris, almost at point blank range by a German, and seriously wounded with five bullets in the leg.) And it seems that I will have the "Medal of the Resistance," but my greatest reward is to know that all my American children are in good health. I know they are all home and that's the main thing.

John, I appreciate your offer and gratefully accept a pair of stockings if it is not hard for you to find them, medium size, and some cigarettes for our sons. This will make you laugh: The Germans were crying out loud when they saw my bare legs in November when it started to get cold. I haven't had stockings for five years. They took everything.

John, my little John, the youngest of my American sons, my regards to you and your parents, and to you a big hug.

Ch. Le Febvre

My grandfather wrote to Russell Cotts a few days later from his airbase—this time in French. He mentioned that he would soon be attending cadet school. He also asked if Russell wouldn't mind sending chewing gum and chocolate, in addition to the stockings and cigarettes Christiane had requested. I was touched by his sign-off, "So long, American friend."

Two months later, shortly after Christiane and her husband returned from leave, she once again wrote to Russell about her impressions of the Germans.

Germany, 6 March 1946

Mon petit Russell,

I often think about my courageous American children who came to save us from the Germans. And I especially think about you, Russell, as you were the youngest, the same age as Claude.

We are back in Germany, but there are so many things we don't have here: we don't always have milk, but they do. Our laundry is gray, but theirs is white. It's ironic: They tortured us and took everything we had, but we can't touch anything of theirs, and they will recover before we do.

Claude is at cadet school and I think he will be successful in aviation. I just adore him. My husband is doing magnificently well after five years in captivity.

My dear Russell, please tell your parents that my home is theirs if they come to France.

With the utmost affection from your French maman.

Ch. Le Febvre

Christiane was back in Rambouillet in May, and she was ecstatic to receive a gift package from the Cotts. She expressed her appreciation in a heartfelt letter.

Rambouillet, 7 May 1946

My dearest friends,

Your gifts have brought me so much joy: stockings, chocolate, cigarettes, soap ... I thank you from the bottom of my heart. It's been six years since I've tasted chocolate, and I will taste only a tiny bit at a time to make it last. France has suffered so: looting, deaths from hunger—misery has made people do bad things.

You've made us so happy. I talk often with Claude about my youngest American son. I loved all my American boys. All I wanted to do was to return them to their parents— because for parents, children are our lives.

My husband and I have just returned from six months in Germany. It was good, but I saw death camps, graves, dead bodies that were burned or buried alive, others shriveled. Poor things. Faces I will never forget.

Our spring is beautiful. Life can be so magnificent.

Once again my faraway friends, thank you from our family to yours. I keep you all close to my heart and for my little Russell, I send kisses from your French maman.

Ch. le Febvre

Every letter written by Christiane and Claude affected me deeply, but this particular one brought back a heartbreaking memory. My maternal grandmother once told me that, during the war, sweets were prohibited. If a person managed to find some chocolate or jam, it was dangerous to share it with children because they might accidentally tell someone they'd eaten the forbidden treat. You might be accused of dealing on the black market, an even more serious offense that could lead to brutal punishment or death. How sad and terrible those times must have been. I'd be torn if I were in a situation like that. Like most children, my Carl loves chocolate. Would I give him the sweet or withhold it? Would my desire to see my son happy overpower my fear of reprisal? I believe my heart would break if I couldn't give my little one a treat for more than six years.

I'm so grateful to live in a society where we are free to do as we wish, one that offers an abundance of choices—which brings me back to my great-grandmother's letter. Reading her words made me realize how fragile our freedoms are, and how important it is to protect them at any cost.

One sentiment Christiane expressed over and over again was her gratitude for the American "children" who had traveled so far to fight for freedom. She understood the sacrifices they had made, and her appreciation was always heartfelt. I love reading her words of thanks. Never for a moment did she take it for granted the fact that young men had come from thousands of miles away so the French could be free.

In that same letter, Christiane shared that Grand-père à Chapeau was looking for work, but he was now fifty-one, so finding a job was difficult. She continued with some good news: Claude had received his *Croix de Guerre* with two silver stars. My great-grandmother also said she'd written to Jack Davis and another American who'd stayed with her, but her letters had been returned.

Claude Le Febvre receives the Croix de Guerre with two silver stars
Rambouillet, France
July 14, 1946

Claude wrote a brief letter to Russell in the month of August as well, half in French and half in English, enthusiastically announcing, "I must go to flying school!" Claude also wrote about his dream of traveling to the United States, but admitted it was probably just a dream. He informed Russell that he and Jeanine would marry when he "had a situation in life," and congratulated Russell on his own engagement.

In the spring of 1947, the Le Febvres sent the Cotts family an invitation to Claude and Jeanine's wedding, but Amy tells me her dad wasn't able to attend. Claude sent a lengthy letter to Russell in May of 1948 and for the first time, it was typewritten—for which Claude apologized. He shared with Russell the joyous news that Jeanine was pregnant and due in September. It seems apparent from Claude's words that Russell had shared the same news about his wife, Doris, in an earlier letter. Claude asked Russell about his studies and jokingly wrote, "Don't you think a semester in a French university, in PARIS for example, would be good for you and Doris?" He ended with, "Please tell us about life in America, the land we like so much without having seen it."

Then in 1956, Christiane sent a brief letter acknowledging the Cotts family's newest member.

Garches, 20 December 1956

My dear Russell,

Another new baby ... little Amy. Congratulations! Such a beautiful family.

As you can see by our address, we've moved. I'm so happy that we're only twenty minutes from Paris.

Claude, Jeanine, and their two sons are doing well. Jeanine is studying to be a dentist.

My dear Russell, I embrace you with all my heart, and thank you for not forgetting me.

Ch. Le Febvre

Their correspondence became less frequent as the years passed (or perhaps some letters were lost), but Christiane continued to thank Russell, calling him her American son, and sometimes even referring to him as her "son who fell from the sky." New Year's and Christmas greetings were exchanged, along with news of children and grandchildren. Claude repeatedly thanked Russell for his friendship and loyalty, and regularly invited him to France. In February of 1962, Claude commented that his father had "stopped everything to take care of Christiane, as she was in poor health." She passed away that same year. Her husband, Grand-père à Chapeau, outlived her by more than two decades.

In September 1964, Russell's younger brother, Bob, visited Claude and Jeanine while he was in Paris for a conference. He wrote a six-page letter to Russell on a Sunday evening, describing his "wonderful night and half-day with the Le Febvres." Grand-père welcomed Bob into his home in Garches (the one I have such fond memories of), and showed him the family photo album, which contained five or six photos of Russell posing with Christiane and the other airmen who were there during that time. Bob commented that he was amazed at how young and boyish Russell appeared in the pictures. My grandfather and Jeanine also took Bob on a tour of Paris, and he saw all the famous landmarks and had a splendid time. Bob wrote, "The only wrong part of the day is that it was me with them instead of you. They look forward to the day when you can visit France. You are the only one from Rambouillet who is still in touch with them."

Almost twenty years after his brother's visit to the Le Febvres, Russell decided to make the journey himself. Grand-père was thrilled.

Wednesday, April 13, 1983

What a nice surprise! We enjoyed receiving your letter and moreover, to know your travel plans. Our house is open as it was in 1944! We are very happy to see you again and to meet Doris.

I have arranged to take vacation days so I can spend time with you. Unfortunately, Jeanine will be in Italy taking a cure for rheumatism.

Please write me all the details regarding your arrival. I am so happy! It was thirty-nine years ago …

My dear American friend, you are still thinking of us, and you are coming to Paris to visit us. It is wonderful.

Very best wishes,

Claude Le Febvre

In one of her emails Amy told me she remembered some of the stories her mom and dad shared after their visit with Grand-père Claude and Jeanine. They talked about a delicious meal of chicken with some unusual mushrooms, and the trip they took to the house in Rambouillet where Christiane and Claude had lived during the war: Unfortunately, no one was home, so they couldn't go in. Amy also said that her dad and Claude laughed and cried over memories of the war.

In the years following the Cotts' visit, my grandparents stayed in touch by sending occasional Christmas greetings to Russell and Doris. The final document was a letter written by my Grandmother Jeanine in 1996, who'd written to inform the Cotts of Grand-père's death. She went on to mention her two sons and her three grandchildren: my brother, my sister, and me. Though she didn't know it at the time she wrote to the Cotts, just a few short weeks later, one her sons, my dad, would also pass away.

The fifty-year relationship that existed between two families separated by six thousand miles could have ended completely with the death of Grand-père Claude, and I'm so grateful it didn't. Amy's letter reaching out to my family following her dad's death rekindled a very important friendship and paved the way for me to gain an understanding of my own ancestors through their letters—correspondence that no one in my immediate family even knew existed.

CHAPTER EIGHTEEN

UNEXPECTED REWARDS

Investigating the past has brought several unexpected rewards. Not only have I been privileged to meet some extraordinary people I may never otherwise have known, my research also has strengthened my relationship with a very special relative, Tante (Aunt) Odette, my great aunt. Tante Odette was Grand-père's sister-in-law, five years younger than her sister, my grandmother Jeanine.

Tante Odette

I suppose I'm not spilling any family secrets when I tell you that at times, Papa had a distant relationship with his mother Jeanine and brother Patrice. He was much closer to his Tante Odette and her only child Valerie, who was about the same age as my papa. The two cousins were constantly together on weekends and holidays— so much so that Tante Odette became like a second mother to Papa. In fact, as I was growing up, Tante Odette was more a grandmother to me than Jeanine was, and Valerie and I also were very attached to one another.

Sadly, almost every older family member dearest to me while I was growing up passed away within a very short period of time: Grand-père, Papa, and Valerie. I've remained close to Tante Odette, now in her eighties, though I believe it sometimes pains her to see me because I look a bit like her beloved Valerie. I've visited my great aunt over the past few months to gather information for my book, and I appreciate how difficult a decision it was for her to assist me: Like many people of her generation who lived through the war, Tante Odette never spoke of her troubling experiences, and probably never would have if I hadn't asked for her help. Tante Odette made it clear to me that she was doing so because she'd loved my papa as if he were her son, but she truly had no desire to rekindle thoughts of that horrible time when her youth was stolen from her. Then she haltingly revealed her memories to me as I probed for answers.

Tante Odette first spoke to me about her recollections when Sascha and I visited her and her husband, Oncle (Uncle) Philippe, on a beautiful spring Sunday afternoon at their home in Versailles. I was touched by the fact that Tante Odette had pulled out an old photo album in preparation for our visit. We talked for a long time and looked at pictures that I'm sure created overwhelming feelings of sadness for my aunt. She also gave me another copy of the *Toutes Les Nouvelles* article, which she had because her brother-in-law, Henri, was the person who'd originally made the connection between the piece in the newspaper and Grand-père. Sascha and I learned many new details about my family that day. Surprisingly, though, we weren't the only ones to hear these things for the first time. Oncle Philippe had been married to Tante Odette for fifty years, and they had a vacation home in Normandy next to Grand-père and Jeanine's vacation home. The two couples had *apéritifs* together every single day. Yet Oncle Philippe had no idea about the Le Febvre family's involvement in the Underground.

We were captivated as Tante Odette talked about Jeanine's activities as a résistant. I hadn't realized how involved she was. Odette remembers Jeanine keeping her armband—which signified her membership in the Underground—in her shoe, and she said Jeanine was heavily involved in scouting the forest for downed airmen.

As Odette spoke, we learned other bits and pieces about my grandparents' lives. It seems the Hôtel du Grand Veneur (a building which exists to this day, though it's now a bank) was owned by the father of Jeanine's best friend's boyfriend. After the liberation of Rambouillet, she and Grand-père spent a great deal of time there with their friends. Of course, I can't help but wonder if they ever met Ernest Hemingway while he was staying there. I like to imagine them sitting around a table engaged in stimulating conversation with the famed author.

I already knew Grand-père had been injured during the liberation of Paris, and Tante Odette told us more about his wounds. She couldn't remember exactly where he was when he was shot—either inside the Sorbonne (a building that housed the University of Paris) or at the Hôtel de Ville (City Hall)—but he had to undergo multiple surgeries on his leg. I'm sure the physical pain he endured was excruciating, and I wonder if the emotional pain of being denied his dream of becoming a pilot was equally agonizing. This had nothing to do with being shot, however. Grand-père was in the Air Force for one year, but according to Tante Odette, his poor eyesight disqualified him from achieving his ambition.

Oncle Philippe, who had to spend most of the war in hiding, took in these disclosures in astonishment, and then shared a little story of his own: As a fifteen-year-old, he used to annoy the Germans by stealing their uniforms and equipment from the beach while they were swimming in the sea! He then proudly produced a photograph of himself posing with a Schmeisser submachine gun.

My second meeting with Tante Odette answered a nagging question. As an adult who'd never lived through war, it was hard for me to understand why no one wanted to talk about their experiences. When I asked her why everyone seemed so reluctant to speak, Odette looked me straight in the eye and said, "No one wants to remember this terrible time. Not only was life difficult during the war, but for several years after when France was being rebuilt. I have happy memories of my early childhood, but I don't like thinking about my teenage years at all." She told me about the day of her confirmation in the Catholic Church. Bombs were exploding all throughout the day; the guests had to take cover and everyone was starving by the time they were able to eat lunch at six o'clock that evening. Odette recalled that her home was near two prime targets, the Kommandantur and the train station. Although no one in her family was injured during the bombing of the train station, they feared for their lives and were forced to leave the house—a terror she'll always remember.

Conditions weren't too bad in Rambouillet during the early days of occupation, Tante Odette claims. Citizens endured a curfew and rationing, but they could obtain extra food through the black market. Residents also managed to peacefully coexist with the Germans, although many weren't happy with the arrangement. Still, their living circumstances were bearable. But as the war wore on, the situation got worse. Tante Odette shudders as she recalls friends of the family disappearing and how speaking to the wrong person or uttering even the most innocent remark could spell doom for an entire family. All it took was an anonymous letter to the Gestapo[22] written by someone who carried a grudge, and lives were turned upside down. Not that they weren't already. Odette especially worried about Christiane, who was a tremendously strong-willed woman. According to her, as far as Christiane's well-being was concerned, the Allies came just in the nick of time, especially since some Rambouillet residents had discovered what was going on at the Le Febvre home.

Odette was twelve years old when Rambouillet was liberated. She says it was one of the most beautiful days of her life: With the arrival of the Americans came the hope of freedom and peace once again. She has fond memories of one particular American, a black man whose name was Jimmy. She said he was incredibly tall and had a gigantic smile. He gave her chocolate and chewing gum.

Although it was difficult for Tante Odette to dig up many of her memories, I'm incredibly grateful she was willing to do so—not only

---

22   The Gestapo was the political police of Nazi Germany.

because it helped me connect the dots about my family, but because of the way our conversations helped strengthen our bond. My journey to the past has helped us reconnect in the present.

Madame L'Allinec

I worked long distance, via telephone and Internet, with Valerie Taloni, an American woman who helped make my dream of writing this book a reality. She was doing some research on the French Resistance, and came across an article that had been published in the *San Francisco Chronicle* on the sixtieth anniversary of D-Day. To learn more about the French Resistance, the journalist who wrote the article had travelled to Rambouillet, where he interviewed two résistants. Valerie excitedly emailed me, suggesting that one of the résistants, Monsieur L'Allinec, might still be alive, and that I should try to locate him. Unfortunately, he passed away a few years ago, but I was able to speak with his widow, Madame Jacqueline L'Allinec, by phone. When I told her I was the great-granddaughter of Christiane Le Febvre, she exclaimed, "Le Febvre … of course I know! They were hiding the pilots. Your great-grandmother was a charismatic woman—she was beautiful with dark hair."

Madame seemed genuinely delighted to hear from me and appeared eager to share her memories. "Madame Le Febvre was hiding the Americans," she said. "She was a smoker, and one day she smoked the American cigarettes the airmen had shared with her from their survival kits right in front of the Germans! Fortunately, they were none the wiser." She also recalled my grandmother Jeanine, and the house in front of the train station, where Jeanine's family had lived. Madame L'Allinec's father-in-law was the director of the hospital and her mother-in-law, the director of the girls' school. Both were part of the "notable society"—and the Underground. I arranged to visit Madame L'Allinec two weeks later.

I met with Madame L'Allinec and her two daughters, Joelle and Laurène, on a Saturday afternoon at Madame's home in Droue-sur-Drouette, a few kilometres from Rambouillet. She was shocked to see the photo of Christiane and the five Americans. Although she knew Christiane was hiding fallen pilots, she had no idea so many were being sheltered at one time, and talked about the incredible risk Christiane had taken. In truth, being a member of the Underground or knowing too much about its activities was so risky, and Madame L'Allinec admitted she knew next to nothing about what her husband did when he was a résistant. Madame knew Monsieur Prompsaud quite well, and said she wished he were still alive to answer my questions about my great-grandmother. I also was pleased to have the opportunity to converse with Laurène, who works for French Public Television and is very knowledgeable about WWII, the French Resistance, and the Allies' involvement, particularly in France. In fact, she worked on a French documentary in 2012 entitled *The English in the Resistance.* Laurène graciously offered me a DVD of her documentary, and I was impressed by the work she'd produced.

The documentary highlighted Britain's contributions to the war effort. One item I learned from the documentary caught me totally off guard, though. When the war ended, our French hero, General de Gaulle, asked those English agents—the same brave men who'd risked their lives to help the French people regain their freedom—to leave France. It may be difficult for some people to understand, but France and England have had an intense love-hate relationship for hundreds of years. I believe we French have underestimated the efforts the British—as well as the Americans and other Allies—made on our behalf during the war, and I'd like to take this opportunity to thank them all.

The L'Allinec family helped me better understand my family's past and my country's history, and I'm grateful to them. We're planning to meet again and I look forward to learning more from them.

Madame Winieska

I have already written about my new friend, Madame Françoise Winieska. She is a remarkable woman whose joie de vivre is infectious. We've had delightfully informative cross-generational conversations, and I've learned so much from her. I always look forward to our discussions.

Amy Cotts Schmidt and Her Family

Amy and I developed a strong bond over the Internet, but I wanted to meet her in person. In the summer of 2015, Sascha and I travelled to Peachtree City, Georgia, where we were welcomed by Amy, her husband John, and their two sons, Nick and Peter. I thought that since we'd never met before, the visit might be a bit awkward at first; but, Sascha and I felt comfortable with the Schmidt family right away. It was as if we were visiting family we hadn't seen for a while. We stayed in their home for two days, and had a splendid time talking about everything under the sun, both past and present. Of course, much of our conversation centered around our families and the war. Amy spoke emotionally about her father, Russell, and she brought out the letters Christiane and Grand-père Claude had written to him. My hands trembled as she placed the letters in them. I had read the copies she had sent to me, but holding the originals moved me to the depths of my soul. As Sascha looked at my father's distinctive signature on one of the letters, he said, "Your signature is very much like his." He was right. Though Sascha had never seen my father's signature, I'd designed my own after his.

I was impressed that Amy had kept all her father's old documents and letters, and Sascha and I were surprised at the large number of WWII veterans' associations in the U.S. We were also astonished that Americans continue to celebrate the war. Even Nick, the Schmidt's twenty-one-year-old son, told me he enjoyed participating in WWII battle re-enactments with his friends and other enthusiasts. We were quite struck by the differences between American and European perceptions of the war. Americans view themselves as the victors and find cause for celebration. We Europeans look back and see a very dark time in our history. Even though, technically, France won in the end, in many ways, we feel we also lost. Our country was split in two as citizen was pitted against citizen—some as collaborators, others as résistants. Lives were lost, homes were destroyed, and our beloved country was left in shambles. Yet despite the many hardships and losses we suffered, we are grateful that the English, the Americans, the other Allied nations, and even the German résistants helped us reclaim our freedom. We just can't celebrate as the Americans do: Even today, the war still brings a bitter taste.

Christiane always considered Russell her "American Son," and by the end of our wonderful visit, I felt such a strong bond of kinship with Amy, I considered her my "American Aunt." Of course, her family became my "American family," and saying good-bye to family is always difficult. But the French have a wonderful saying—"à bientôt," which means "see you soon." And we will.

THE PRICE OF FREEDOM

The first time I gave any thought to the notion of freedom, I was twelve years old. It was July 14, 1989, and my country was commemorating the two hundredth anniversary of the French Revolution, which gave birth to our national motto: "Liberté-Egalité-Fraternité" ("Liberty-Equality-Fraternity"). I wanted to celebrate the bicentennial by doing my part, so I replaced my normal shoelaces with ones that were the same colors as the French flag: blue, white, and red. I proudly sported those colorful laces—and in my young mind, my patriotism—the entire day. Looking back, I see how naïve I was, not only in the manner in which I chose to celebrate our national holiday, but in my understanding of the concept of freedom.

Having the opportunity to travel from a young age has helped broaden my horizons, and I realize I'm lucky—privileged really—to have been able to journey to diverse locations. As a French citizen, visas are fairly simple to obtain, so I have the freedom to move from one country to another with relative ease. Traveling is a passion of mine, and I never tire of experiencing new places.

I visited Syria a few years ago, before it was devastated by its civil war. The country was one of the most beautiful places I'd ever been—so rich in its people, culture, and history. Palmyra was an archaeological jewel, and Aleppo contained the largest covered market in the world. I adored both cities and spent hours exploring them. However, I also discovered that, behind the country's breath-taking treasures was a stark reality: the absence of freedom. This came as a shock to me. Sure, like everyone else in the free world, I'd been bombarded with news from around the globe about dictatorial societies and repressed populations, about people who are fighting for liberty, or perhaps worst of all, have no recourse but to live in a society where they can do nothing but suffer without hope of ever gaining their freedom. But, because it was happening to someone else and not me, I never gave those stories serious thought. As a French woman, my freedom was guaranteed. Or at least I thought it was.

Now I know better. Just because you're French, or British, or American—or from any other country that values and safeguards freedom—doesn't mean your freedom is guaranteed to last forever. Less than a lifetime ago, my own relatives—in fact, all my countrymen—had the unthinkable happen: Almost every liberty they possessed was taken from them, including the ability to keep the food they grew, buy necessities, savor a piece of chocolate, wear stockings, walk down the street at any hour they pleased, retain their possessions, and for some, even the ability to live in their own homes. The world they once knew no longer existed. But brave men and women joined together in the spirit of resistance and fought to regain their freedom. And, they were joined by thousands of men like Jack Davis and Russell Cotts—fellows so young they were closer to boyhood than to manhood—who came to help them win this battle.

If I ever have to fight to keep the freedom given to us by the previous generation, I believe I will. To be honest, though, no one ever really knows how they'd react in those circumstances, and I think it's best to try not to judge those who've been faced with that decision.

A popular French song, "Né en 17 à Leidenstadt," ("Born in 1917 in Leidenstadt"), captures my attitude. In this song, composer Jean-Jacques Goldman (a French Jew) underlines the fact that it's easy to judge, though we never know how we will react in a given situation. (The song's lyrics are included on the last page of this book, along with the English translation.) Americans had no doubts regarding which side of the conflict they had to choose in WWII. But for Europeans, it wasn't that easy: Some chose National Socialism for ideological reasons, or because they believed it would protect them from Communism. Others followed Hitler simply because they were German, or because they saw it as a way to protect their families. Even today, children and grandchildren of Nazis bear the fault of their ancestors, even though the war ended more than seven decades ago. Instead of placing judgment, perhaps we can ask ourselves what we can do during our lifetime to maintain the freedoms our ancestors fought so hard to protect: "What can we do to preserve the freedom we now enjoy—for ourselves and our children?"

Sascha and I live in Berlin, a city that was the center of the Third Reich. Of course, I'd always heard of the Berlin Wall—the great divide, constructed in 1961—but I never understood its history. The Communist government of East Germany said the wall's purpose was to keep Western fascists from entering East Germany and undermining the socialist state. In reality, the main objective was to stop the mass defections from East to West. In other words, it was built to deny freedom.

Two years after the Berlin Wall's construction, American President John F. Kennedy visited Berlin. There, on June 26, 1963, he made his famous speech from the Rathaous Schöneberg, which concludes with "Ich bin ein Berliner" ("I am a Berliner"), underlining the United States' support of West Germany and disdain for Communism. He challenged those—who didn't understand why living in a free society was such a big deal—to look to the divided city of Berlin as an example:

> There are many people in the world who really don't understand, or say they don't, what is the great issue between the free world and the Communist world. Let them come to Berlin.

There are some who say that Communism is the wave of the future. Let them come to Berlin. And there are some who say in Europe and elsewhere we can work with the Communists. Let them come to Berlin. And there are even a few who say that it is true that Communism is an evil system, but it permits us to make economic progress. Lass'sie nach Berlin kommen. Let them come to Berlin.[23]

Even living in Schöneberg, Berlin's former American district (not far from where JFK made his famous speech), I'd never given much thought to the wall, which was torn down in 1989—just a generation ago. That changed one morning in November 2014, when I was escorting Carl to kindergarten. We boarded our usual bus, which traveled from west to east within the city. Just a few minutes into our journey, I looked out the window in the direction where the wall once stood. What an amazing sight! Instead of concrete, there was a wall of balloons. It had been created to celebrate the twenty-fifth anniversary of the fall of the Berlin Wall. Overwhelmed with what I'd seen, I dropped Carl off at school, and chatted with another mother who was about my age. She told me she'd grown up in East Germany and choked up as she described her memories. "I was a teenager when the wall fell, and suddenly I was free for the first time. I met my husband, who had grown up on the other side of the wall, after the wall came down. If the wall was still there, I can't imagine what my life would be like. I am grateful for my freedom every single day."

Sascha and I attended the magnificent celebration of this historic event—a celebration of freedom. Thousands of illuminated balloons stood in place of the old barrier. It was spectacular.

In the same month that I began working on this book, terrorists forced their way into the offices of *Charlie Hebdo*, a satirical weekly Parisian newspaper, and brutally murdered eleven people: another reminder that our freedoms can be challenged at any given moment. I was proud to see citizens of France—indeed, people throughout the

---

23   John F. Kennedy Presidential Library and Museum. The Cold War in Berlin. Retrieved from http://www.jfklibrary.org/JFK/JFK-in-History/The-Cold-War-in-Berlin.aspx

free world—stand in support of these fallen men and women. That gives me hope … hope that future generations will learn from the courageous actions of others, including the people in this book, and never allow someone to take away their liberty or allow others' lives to be taken on the basis of beliefs or nationality.

President Kennedy essentially said in 1963 that people didn't understand what it means to live without freedom—that it was taken for granted. That was certainly my reality just a short time ago. And while I've never experienced the absence of freedom, I now have more of an understanding. It's been an ongoing process, but my thinking has evolved quite a bit. I know this: We cannot take our freedom for granted, and we must preserve it.The Swiss watchmaker Patek Philippe has a slogan, "You never actually own a Patek Philippe watch, you merely look after it for the next generation." I now feel this way about the liberty I enjoy, and will never again take freedom for granted.

And as for Christiane never receiving her medal … I have not been able to determine why. Just recently, when preparing to have her garage painted, Maman found another file. It contained the bottom part of the half-note, in which its author continued to plead the case for Christiane to receive an award from France. The letter was not signed. I've discovered that even Monsieur Prompsaud, who hired my great-grandmother into the French Resistance, had advocated on her behalf. Regretfully, he retired from politics immediately after the end of the war, as he was unhappy with the new French government. Perhaps, if he hadn't retired, he would have continued to push for Christiane's award. But it no longer matters to me: My great-grandmother didn't fight for glory—or a medal. She fought for freedom. Christiane's honesty, courage, and adherence to her values despite the risks have made her not only my hero, but also my example.

It is my hope that Christiane's courage—and that of the airmen she housed—will also serve as a model for my son to follow. I had to learn about my family's fight for freedom from a woman across the Atlantic, but I want Carl to hear about it from his mother, through the example of his ancestors. Our son has been my motivation to write my family's story: Without him, it would have remained, in pieces, in a drawer.

I want Carl to know not only who he is, but also how his family's story fits into the larger narrative of history. For our son and for all of us, a grasp of the past is key to understanding the world today. Only then can we truly value the freedom we have and be willing to fight to preserve it at any cost.

Christiane Le Febvre Receiving the U.S. Medal of Freedom
January 18, 1947
Paris, France

The President
OF THE UNITED STATES OF AMERICA
has directed me to express to

CHRISTIANE LEFEBVRE

*the gratitude and appreciation of the
American people for gallant service
in assisting the escape of Allied
soldiers from the enemy*

DWIGHT D. EISENHOWER
General of the Army
Commanding General United States Forces European Theater

Certificate that accompanied Christiane Le Febvre's Medal of Freedom

ACKNOWLEDGMENTS

This is the most difficult and important part of my book, and I hope I haven't left anyone out.

Throughout this incredible quest, I've been fortunate to meet and work with some of the most generous and amazing people who've helped me in more ways than I ever thought possible. I'm not sure I can adequately express my thanks to everyone, but without them I never could have undertaken this wonderful project.

I believe an angel above has guided my journey from the very first moment, helping me find the missing pieces of the puzzle and steering me in the right directions.

Sascha, thank you for planting the seeds of this project in my mind. You helped and encouraged me every step of the way, so this book is yours as much as it is mine.

This book never would have been written without Amy Cotts Schmidt. With one gesture, a short, simple letter, she altered my life and motivated me to seek out my family's truth. Along the way, we exchanged letters and emails, and she provided documents, photos, and insights that assisted me as I journeyed through the past.

Thank you to every organization, family, and individual who shared information, advice, and words of wisdom, comfort, and encouragement, including:

BARBIER: Pierre
BARON: Gerald
BERINSTAIN: Odette, Philippe
BOURREE: Fabrice
CALLIES: Jacques
CHARRIER: Patrick
CHAUDRON: Agathe
COMET LINE
CORNEVIN: Didier
DAVIS: Jimmy
DORSEY: Mike
D'OULTREMONT: Brigitte
DREVET: Cyril
DUBOIS: Aurore
EMERSON: John, Kimberly
FOHLEN WEILL: Gerard
FONTAINE: Thomas
GOLDMAN: Jean-Jacques
GROMIER: Florence
GROSBOIS: Alexis
GUERIN: Jean-Paul
INGLIS: Tess, Ann, Don
KATSAROS: John
KHAIAT: Gilles
KUŠEJ: Martin
L'ALLINEC: Jacqueline, Joelle, Laurène
LAMBERT: Maud, Lionel, Lucie, Manon
LANDSHOFF: Antje
LARCHER: Gerard

LE FEBVRE: Maman, Yann, Alexandra, Teva, Lola, Atea
McDONNELL: Aoife
MORAN: Darren
PELOILLE: François
PRIMOSCH: Ernst
REXROTH: Olga
SANCHEZ: Ana
SCHMIDT: Amy, John, Peter, Nick
SENFFT: Heinrich
SHARY
TAILLEFERD: Caroline
TALONI: Valerie, Adam
TAVAINE: Bernard, Madeleine
U.S. Air Force Escape and Evasion Society
URBAN: Britta
VENTURINO: Marie-Laure
VONHIR: Christoph
WINIESKA: Françoise

Thank you to the innovative geniuses who've created online databases, websites, libraries, blogs, documentaries, archives, and all the tools that made the search much easier. The Internet with all of its amazing sites, from YouTube to Facebook, helped make this book possible. Unbelievable as it may seem, I even found a hand-written copy of Christiane's 1889 birth certificate online.

And to you, the reader, thank you.

Marie

ABOUT THE AUTHOR

A perfumer and pilot, Marie began to explore her family's exciting past in 2010. She continues to delve into history, particularly how it relates to peace and freedom in the world today.

In 2014 Marie moved with her husband, Sascha, and their son, Carl, from Paris to Berlin, where they fulfilled their dream of opening a perfume laboratory and launching their own "Urban Scents" brand of fragrances (www.UrbanScents.de). Her journey into her family's past influences her work as she sources ingredients that help provide income for people impacted by economic and political unrest. She's currently developing "Utopia," a scent that blends materials from around the world, including elements from countries at odds with one another. This fragrance is her personal expression of peace.

CONNECT WITH THE AUTHOR

Please visit www.RiskingAndResisting.com, where you can connect with the author, view copies of the original documents and photos, and comment on her blog.

BIBLIOGRAPHY

Chapter 3

Bolinger, Bruce C. (n.d.). Comet Line (Le Réseau Comète). Retrieved from http://wwii-netherlands-escape-lines.com/other-escape-lines/comet-line-le-reseau-comete/

Désenclos, S. (1988, April 8). Forty-Four Years Later, Fate Brings Them Together. *Toutes Les Nouvelles*.

Spotts, Frederic. (2010). Oh, What a Lovely War! *In The Shameful Peace: How French Artists and Intellectuals Survived the Nazi Occupation.* Retrieved from https://books.google.com/books?id=HSBiE6g9VV4C&pg=PT45&lpg=PT45&dq=rambouillet+during+german+occupation&source=bl&ots=cpmTu5F-qN&sig=q2MHUuiNsIllaqmUBJi-kjPTUyA&hl=en&sa=-X&ei=-zdeVZa3O8G4sAWujYD4BA&ved=0CDoQ6AEwBA#v=onepage&q=rambouillet%20during%20german%20occupation&f=false

Chapter 4

Armistice of 11 November 1918. (2015). Retrieved from http://www.france.fr/en/institutions-and-values/armistice-11-november-1918.html

D-Day Memorial Foundation. (2013). D-Day Overview. Retrieved from https://www.dday.org/history/d-day-the-invasion/overview

Combined Operations Command. (2000-2015). Operations Neptune and Overlord. Retrieved from http://www.combinedops.com/Overlord.htm

George Washington University. World War II (1939-1945). *The Eleanor Roosevelt Papers Project*. Retrieved from http://www.gwu.edu/~erpapers/teachinger/glossary/world-war-2.cfm

History. (2015). World War I History. Retrieved from http://www.history.com/topics/world-war-ii/world-war-i-history

History. (2015). World War II History. Retrieved from http://www.history.com/topics/world-war-ii/world-war-ii-history

The Library of Congress. (n.d.). D-Day June 6, 1944. America's Story from America's Library. Retrieved from http://www.americaslibrary.gov/jb/wwii/jb_wwii_dday_3.html

National Geographic Society. (2015). Pearl Harbor World War II Timeline. Retrieved from http://www.nationalgeographic.com/pearlharbor/history/wwii_timeline.htmlp

The National WWII Museum. (n.d.). D-Day: June 6, 1944:. Retrieved from http://www.nationalww2museum.org/learn/education/for-students/ww2-history/d-day-june-6-1944.html

Simons, Marlise. (1995, July 17). Chirac Affirms France's Guilt in Fate of Jews. *The New York Times*. Retrieved from http://www.nytimes.com/1995/07/17/world/chirac-affirms-france-s-guilt-in-fate-of-jews.html

Smith, Meredith. (2010). *The Civilian Experience in German-Occupied France, 1940-1944.* Retrieved from http://digitalcommonsconcoll.edu/histhp/6

Treaty of Versailles 1919. (n.d.). In *Holocaust Encyclopedia.* Retrieved from http://www.ushmm.org/wlc/en/article.php?ModuleId=10005425

U.S. Department of State. (n.d.). Milestones 1914-1920. Retrieved from https://history.state.gov/milestones/1914-1920/paris-peace

Wichers, Shannon. (Summer 2011). The Forgotten Victims of the North: French Civilians under German Occupation during World War I. *Armstrong Undergraduate Journal of History* 1, no.2

Chapter 11

Charles de Gaulle Foundation. (n.d.). *Appel du 18 Juin 1940 du General de Gaulle.* Retrieved from http://www.charles-de-gaulle. org/pages/l-homme/dossiers-thematiques/1940-1944-la-seconde-guerre-mondiale/l-appel-du-18-juin/documents/l-appel-du-18-juin-1940.php

The French Resistance. (n.d.). Retrieved from http://www.scrapbookpages.com/Natzweiler/History/FrenchResistance.html

Lava Development, LLC. (2004-2015). Charles de Gaulle. *World War II Database.* Retrieved from http://ww2db.com/person_bio. php?person_id=68

Lava Development, LLC. (2004-2015). The French Resistance. World War II Database. Retrieved from http://ww2db.com/battle_spec.php?battle_id=153

Miele, Dan. (2008, March 10). *The French Resistance: The Silent Heroes of WWII.* Retrieved from https://www.youtube.com/watch?v=b41mliPt0Xo

Rousso, Henry. (1987). *Le Syndrome de Vichy: de 1944 à nos jours.* Paris: Editions du Seuil.

Trueman, Chris. (2000-2015). *The French Resistance.* Retrieved from http://www.historylearningsite.co.uk/french_resistance.htm

Williams, Michael. (March 2000-May 2015.) *Oradour-sur-Glane 10th June 1944.* Retrieved from http://www.oradour.info

Chapter 15

Comète Kinship Belgium. (n.d.). *Aviateurs alliés rassemblés en camps de Comète.* Retrieved from http://www.cometeline.org/ficheD372.html

Chapter 16

History. (2015). *Aug 25, This Day in History.* Retrieved from http://www.history.com/this-day-in-history/liberation-of-paris

Le Parisien. (2014, August 19). *La Difficile Entrée des Américains dans Rambouillet.* Retrieved from http://www.leparisien.fr/espace-premium/yvelines-78/

Rickard, J. (2009, May 28). Leonard Townsend Gerow, 1888-1972. In *Military History Encyclopedia on the Web.* Retrieved from http://www.historyofwar.org/articles/people_gerow_leonard.html

Taylor, Lois. (1997, July 18). Gardens of France. *Honolulu Star-Bulletin.* Retrieved from http://archives.starbulletin.com/97/07/22/features/evergreen.html

Trueman, Chris. *The Liberation of Paris.* Retrieved from http://www.historylearningsite.co.uk/

Winieska, Francoise. (1999). *August 1944: The Liberation of Rambouillet, France.* Rambouillet, France: SHARY.

Chapter 18

Gestapo. (2015). In Encyclopædia Britannica. Retrieved from http://www.britannica.com/topic/Gestapo

The Price of Freedom

Goldman, Jean-Jacques. (1990). Né en 17 à Leidenstadt [song lyrics]. In Fredericks Goldman Jones. Retrieved from http://lyricstranslate.com/en/n%C3%A9-en-17-%C3%A0-leidenstadt-born-1917-leidenstadt.html

John F. Kennedy Presidential Library and Museum. (n.d.) The Cold War in Berlin. Retrieved from http://www.jfklibrary.org/JFK/JFK-in-History/The-Cold-War-in-Berlin.aspx

History. (2015). Berlin Wall. Retrieved from http://www.history.com/topics/cold-war/berlin-wall

NÉ EN 17 À LEIDENSTADT

Né en 17 à Leidenstadt[24]

Et si j'étais né en 17 à Leidenstadt
Sur les ruines d'un champ de bataille
Aurais-je été meilleur ou pire que ces gens
Si j'avais été allemand ?

Bercé d'humiliation, de haine et d'ignorance
Nourri de rêves de revanche
Aurais-je été de ces improbables consciences
Larmes au milieu d'un torrent ?

Si j'avais grandi dans les docklands de Belfast
Soldat d'une foi, d'une caste
Aurais-je eu la force envers et contre les miens
De trahir: tendre une main

---

24   Included with the permission of JRG Editions Musicales.

Si j'étais née blanche et riche à Johannesburg
Entre le pouvoir et la peur
Aurais-je entendu ces cris portés par le vent
Rien ne sera comme avant

On saura jamais c'qu'on a vraiment dans nos ventres
Caché derrière nos apparences
L'âme d'un brave ou d'un complice ou d'un bourreau?
Ou le pire ou le plus beau ?
Serions-nous de ceux qui résistent ou bien les moutons d'un troupeau
S'il fallait plus que des mots ?

Et si j'étais né en 17 à Leidenstadt
Sur les ruines d'un champ de bataille
Aurais-je été meilleur ou pire que ces gens
Si j'avais été allemand ?

Et qu'on nous épargne à toi et moi
si possible très longtemps
D'avoir à choisir un camp

Born in 17 in Leidenstadt

And if I were born in '17 in Leidenstadt
On the ruins of a battlefield
Would I have been better or worse than those people,
If I had been German?

Nursed with humiliation, hatred, and ignorance
Fed with dreams of revenge
Would I have been one of those improbably aware people
Tears in a river?

Had I grown up in the docklands of Belfast
One time soldier, on one side
Would I have had the strength to betray my people,
Stretch my hand?

If I'd been born white and rich in Johannesburg
Between power and fear
Would I have heard those cries carried by the wind,
Nothing will be like before

We will never know what we really have in our guts
Hidden behind appearances
A brave's, an accomplice's, a torturer's soul?
Or the worst or the most beautiful one?
Would we be like those who resist, or the sheep following the herd
If more than words were needed?

And if I were born in '17 in Leidenstadt
On the ruins of a battlefield
Would I have been better or worse than those people,
If I had been German?

But I would like you and me to be spared
For a long time if possible
From having to choose one side.

www.ingramcontent.com/pod-product-compliance
Lightning Source LLC
Chambersburg PA
CBHW060758050426
42449CB00008B/1442